The
Football Handbook
to end all
Football Handbooks

The
Football Handbook
to end all
Football Handbooks

CHRIS LIGHTBOWN

Jacket illustration by Derek Alder
Other illustrations by Paul Rigby

WOLFE PUBLISHING LIMITED

First published 1974 by
Wolfe Publishing Limited
10 Earlham Street
London WC2H 9LP

SBN 7234 0532 8

Printed by The Garden City Press Limited
Letchworth, Hertfordshire SG6 1JS

*To all the great people I met through Football, including:
Eric, Eamonn, Eddy, Peter, Rolo, Bradford Peter, Vinny,
Tommy Murphy, Sideways, Jugwood, Leeds Skin, Little
Martin, Big Les, Steve and Vic, Bernard, Mick, Goosey,
Ray, Dave P., John, Andy, Steve, Charlton Andy, and to
Dave, who knows nothing about football, but who is my mate.*

Contents

CHAPTER ONE

Pre-Match Kickabout

EVEN before publication, the Publishers have received thousands of letters from football fans the world over, applauding the *Football Handbook To End All Football Handbooks*. Typical, is this letter from Mr. Agitated, of Indignant, Surrey.

I have read your unwarranted little diatribe, laughingly entitled The Football Handbook To End All Football Handbooks, *and find it quite the most distasteful piece of literature yet to cross my threshold. Not only is it a comprehensive examination of all the parts of football, including those that are none of your business, but it omits to mention a number of important and vitally necessary people involved in the game, including notably, myself.*

Furthermore, although I wish to make it clear that there is no question of sour grapes, I failed all of the competitions in the book, and found them both extortionate, and devious in their conception. I am sure my friends at the Headquarters of the Committee of Pompous People in Charge of Football, will take a dim view of this whole sorry episode, and as soon as I can locate their address somewhere or other in the heart of the Lancashire countryside, I will be writing to them to notify them of this disgusting business.

And furthermore, the Referee's decision referred to on Page 616 was quite the worst case of refereeing I have ever come across in 43 years of football watching. The player was clearly offside. I was there at the time, so don't argue. And in addition, I unhesitatingly refute your slanderous accusation, made repeatedly in the book, that no one in football understands the Offside Law. I do. And I enclose a diagram of the incident I refer to above. Such abysmal ignorance on your part, is no excuse for anticipating similar ignorance in others more versed in the sport than you are.

This correspondence is now closed. My 14-year-old son found your book very informative and interesting. Which shows you how bad it must be. He, certainly, knows absolutely nothing about the Offside Law.

Yours, etc.

JRS Agitated, (Mrs. Major), Indignant, Surrey.

Well how about that folks!! People have been dying to write to us even before the book came out on the market! The book that no self-respecting Psychologist would be without!! And as the competitions, in particular, have proved so popular, we are going to run an additional one at this point in the book: If *you* hated *The Football Handbook To End All Football Handbooks*, just write your reasons for not liking the book in not less than 12,000 words, in a defensive formation, with two Forwards and a Sweeper, and send them along with seven of the easy-to-tear-off coupons from the corner of Chapter 8, and lots of money, to Chrisn'Paul, Laughingallthewaytothebank, Skylark, Bermuda.

Pompous Introduction By Chris Lightbown

SOMETIMES, people come up to me in the street, ordinary, simple, everyday people, and ask me what it was that moved me to write this book. I tell them that I think we people in football have an obligation to explain various facets of the game to outsiders who must be quite baffled by what they have heard in recent years of our National Sport.

Is it true, they may well feel, for example, that Football has become overwhelmed with Sociologists, Skinheads, Psychiatrists, Psychologists, Social Workers, Do-Gooders, Ticket Touts, Film Stars and Shotgun-Wielding Maniacs, and that there is no longer any room in the game for people who just want to kick a ball around for 90 or so minutes? Other people ask me if it is true, as some have suggested, that Football is one massive con trick, perpetuated by a horde of unscrupulous Agents, Chairmen, Toilet Roll Manufacturers and Hot Dog Salesmen. Some people go even further, and ask me if I think that our whole existence has come to revolve around Football; whether it is only a matter of time before our children are required to learn the Offside Law by heart, and all able-bodied men are conscripted as Skinheads.

I tell people that it is my great concern for the issues raised in these searching questions, and my intrinsic feeling that we in The Game have an obligation to answer such queries, that has led me to write this book. Then again, I am sometimes honest, and I tell them that I wrote it for the money.

What They Said About The Football Handbook To End All Football Handbooks

Diamond 'Anybody's' Lil, 414 Dagenham Road, Dockside:
"I like it."

The Hon. Lord Wilcox of Knickers:
"I am one of the self-righteous and pompous people who get asked to write self-righteous and pompous Introductions to all sorts of books. I am often to be found on the inside cover of Football Programmes, too, making self-righteous and pompous Introductions there, as well.

I don't really know why I have been asked to give an Introduction to this book, as it does not seem as stuffy and pretentious as the books one normally lends one's name to (for £15 a time, if anyone is interested; £20 if you want an attack on modern youth and values, thrown in).

Still, I had better say all the normal things one says on these occasions, or one won't get one's fee.

I have read this book very carefully, and I believe that it is making a vital and very important statement about all the things that we consider to be important in this modern day and age. In these difficult times, when all the values of civilisation, as we know it, are being threatened as never before, it is indeed reassuring to be presented with a volume such as this one.

It is the purpose of Sport to bring together men of different races and nationalities in one true bond of brotherhood and sportsmanship. In such an atmosphere, it is possible for us human beings to discover the common bond that truly links us, whatever our diverse circumstances, and thus through Sport, forge a bond of common humanity that shall overcome all difficulties.

It is to encourage these values, of comradeship, universal, brotherhood, self-assurance, fidelity, and true sportsmanship, that men come together in sporting activities the world over, and wherever they do so, it is indeed gratifying to think that there are books like this, to draw us, the uninvolved bystanders, closer into the great human intercourse that characterises all such activities. We are most privileged to have such a talented, worthy and timely reminder of the values of such activities in this modern day and age, where one increasingly finds as never before, that the values one knows and accepts . . ."

(Continued in Next Edition.)

Jed. J. Jerkoff III, rich American from Phoenix, Arizona, who likes to buy things English, cut them into little pieces, and have them shipped back to his ranch in the States:
"My wife Martha and I have thoroughly enjoyed this book, and would very much like to have it broken up into little pieces and exported back to the States, where we will re-build it next to your very own London Bridge. We think your Policemen are wonderful."

The Skull End: (4,000 voices, all in unison)
"What a load of rubbish!"

A. J. R. Thingame, Spokesman for the Committee of Pompous People in Charge of Football
"Books such as this bring The Game into disrepute, and threaten the very fabric of The Game, and of civilisation as we know it. The Committee has decided to fine this book £50, and ban it for six months."

Arthur Knowlesworth-Blair, Chairman, Ham United Football Club
"I am a very important person."

The Daily Splurge
"Young Football Superstar in Sex Orgy Heartbreak Bunny Girl Transfer Shock Drama Sensation."

Jed. J. Jerkoff III:
"My wife Martha and I, have been very impressed with Chris Lightbown/Paul Rigby, and would like to buy them up, chop them into little pieces, ship them across the Atlantic, and re-build them in our little plot of land there, right next door to your very own English country pub that we bought on the last occasion."

AUTHOR!
AUTHOR!!
KILL IM!
F.A. CUP
FOOTBALL HANDBOOKS
THE FOOTBALL HANDBOOK TO END ALL

CHAPTER TWO

Origins Of Football

Great, Free "Origins of Football" Wallchart offer, exclusive to readers of the Football Handbook To End All Football Handbooks! Trace Man's progress from the seas —to swamps—to primeval forests—to football pitches, with this magnificent easy-to-use Wallchart!

Recall the days when referees were apes swinging through the trees, and full backs rode into battle on the backs of dinosaurs! Hours of fun!

Did you know who the world's first football hooligan was? Do you know what he told the magistrate? Do you know why Napoleon really invaded Russia—that it was really a scouting trip to check out a promising young Omsk Rovers wing half?

These, and thousands of other useless facts will be at your finger tips, or anywhere else you care to put them, if you send 16 dust covers of the Football Handbook To End All Handbooks, *a list of League Champions from 1450 to the present day and £75, to Football Wallchart Offer, (Mugs I), Uncle Sid's Dirty Bookshop, Porno Terrace, Suffolk. Satisfaction guaranteed, or your dustcovers returned.*

FOOTBALL, like all sports, has its roots in the very heart and fabric of our civilisation and history. Football arises from the thickest mists of antiquity (thickest being the operative word).

It is one of man's basic instincts; after the instinct to eat, drink and have it off repeatedly with naked ladies, nothing comes closer to a man's heart than the feel of studs on flesh, of kicking the hell out of his fellow man. And this is the noble purpose served by football. (It is also served, occasionally, by other things like war, massacres and muggings, substitute activities for football; more about that later.)

There is nothing so pleasing to a man as the feel of his studs biting into another man's vitals; or if he is a spectator, of pummelling the living daylights out of other spectators. Unmanly men and cowards seek refuge in timid roles such as TV commentators, referees, linesmen, programme sellers, journalists, writers of silly books about football; these are lesser breeds of men, and are generally despised by all Men worthy of the name.

Indeed, football arises from the very core of our being, it is the essence of the spirit of Man. More specifically, football, like all our sports, arose from the time when it was the practice to behead social misfits and put their heads to profitable use in the community.

The First Footballs

The basic concept of football first arose in Ancient Britain, which was a very basic place, with the Dim tribe who beheaded all unsuccessful tribal warriors returning from battle. They then used the heads as rudimentary balls in a rudimentary game of football, played with rudimentary rules and a very rudimentary referee. The advantage of using heads as footballs was of course, that wherever men met for a game and no football was available, they could make one of their own on the spot. Spectators drew lots for the privilege; one of the many quaint early football traditions now carried on by the Skinheads.

If any lily-livered member of the tribe found any of this distasteful, he was allowed to put in a request for a transfer to the Even-Dimmer Tribe in the North of Britain, where the practice was to behead fighting failures, and use the heads instead, as catapult missiles. The trajectory of these missiles led to streamlined heads, sliplinc heads and the game of Rugby (see Handbook).

The practice was stamped out by the Romans when they took over Britain, in a massive transfer deal to stop this country being relegated, which was a very real possibility at the time; "I came, I saw, I moved the left back to inside right" (Jock Caesar, Anglo Roman Team Manager, 55 Seasons BC). Nearly all English football teams are managed by Scots, and no team is complete without a few vicious Celts. This arises from one of the lesser known Clauses of the Act of Union between England and Scotland, widely referred to among historians as "The Clause in the Act of Union that says there must be at least three Scots players in every English football team, and the teams should all have Scottish Managers". In return, Scotland promised never to qualify for the World Cup, and to stop sending raiding parties of Skinheads over Hadrian's Wall to attack innocent English Season Ticket Holders.

It was the Roman practice to behead rebellious Britons and put the heads on spears, which were then placed along the public highway, where members of the public were invited to vent their spleen whilst travelling (see Handbook on Darts). Decapitated heads also came into use in road building, a major Roman hobby when not empire building. They were used for rolling along the ground to determine the flatness of the surface (see Handbook on Bowling).

The Romans, who also played rudimentary games of football, adopted and eventually modified the old British idea of using random heads as rudimentary footballs. (It was around this time that the Italian referee was invented, a black day for football.) Young children also found the heads useful as toy weapons and playthings (see Handbooks on Conkers, Cricket, Tennis, Baseball, etc. etc. etc.).

However, with the advent of the Beheading Superstar, who

mounted the scaffold waving a 24-clause contract, with Repeat, Copyright and Performing Rights drawn up for each possible use of his head, and the inflationary effect of multi-purpose cut-price Japanese heads flooding the market, it was recognised that things had gone too far and that the Game would have to be amended.

So the Rudimentary Committee of Pompous People in Charge of Rudimentary Football, were woken up and asked to consider proposals for the introduction of a non-human, automated football. After much head-shaking, and admonishing of "This tinkering with the very concept of the game . . ."; "What are things coming to when . . ."; "Football has existed perfectly well on heads for centuries now . . ."; they duly passed the proposals, and went back to sleep for another three and a half centuries.

Enter The Skinheads

The Roman Empire, and hence, their system of football, ended with the invasion of the Huns and Skinheads, two primitive tribes from Central Asia, who believed in playing football without a referee. The period that followed came to be known as the Dark Ages, because there were no floodlit games in this period, and also there were many foul nasties done to people, even more than before, and almost as many as the present day. After the Skinheads had sacked Rome, they travelled across the length of Europe, on Football Specials, pillaging and plundering as they went.

Whole stands were razed to the ground, goalkeepers were hanged from their own goalposts, Hot Dog Sellers were roasted in their own Hot Dog stands and talented ball players were torn apart by sharpened steel combs, and left rotting on the terraces. There were days when skilled players sought refuge in monasteries, coaching the monks, and eventually dedicated their lives to painting illuminated match programmes and stained glass turnstiles.

Gradually, the Skinheads came to dominate all Europe, except for a little bit around the Streatham area, which they left alone for reasons best known to themselves. Little pockets of resistance, where bunches of referees and linesmen had gone into hiding were slowly snuffed out, while entertaining football aesthetes who had gone to ground with their edited highlights of entertaining Matches-of-the-Day, were winkled out by posses of Skinheads on "Search and Destroy" missions, and their television recordings publicly destroyed. Wembley Stadium was turned into a massive monument to the Skinheads' alien God, Booto, God of Bovver. They raped the women, drank the wine, and wrecked every Football Special in sight.

The effect on football was traumatic; defensive football became the order of the day, and it was to be many centuries before a brave man would again venture to play attacking football. Centre forwards the world over feared for their lives, as well as for the safety of their Bunny Girls.

Gradually, the Skinheads settled down, and slowly became nicer people. Then, because that was not at all what they wanted to be, they decided to invent wars with other countries. So they attacked the Moors in the Middle East, in a fruitless series of attempts to recover the World Cup from Jerusalem.

It was a time when the Game of Football fell into disrepute, and, some would say, it has remained there ever since.

Football has, of course, existed hundreds of years BC (Before Cops), but it did not realise its potential for mayhem and unadulterated human misery and suffering, until the emergence of the Skinheads.

After a few centuries of this, the Skinheads got bored; they were rapidly running out of people to attack and bovver to make. There was also at this time, a crisis of supply and demand in the toilet roll industry (more later). So they went back whence they came, commonly believed to be a dung heap just outside Birmingham, and reserved their appearances for Saturday afternoons at football matches.

Wars Take Over

The practice of holding wars and invading other peoples' countries, and drinking their wine, and raping their naked ladies, had in fact existed for several centuries BC. The tradition arose, of course, from European football competitions, where clubs that had done well in their own country's competitions went and played similarly successful sides in Europe, often not getting back until the early hours of the morning. In this you will recognise the origin of National Service—everyone who is fit in body but not in mind, goes off and fights the foreigners.

Football became so bloodthirsty, that after a time, when the Committee of Pompous People in Charge of Football were not watching, it became necessary to invent a substitute activity to use up the energy that people were using in football, but which would not do so much damage. So wars were invented. But the only really satisfactory wars that went far enough to be true substitutes for football, were the two World Wars. (The other advantage of having wars instead, is that it gave the sociologists a break from analysing football hooligans, and gave them instead, a host of subjects to drool over for years afterwards.) After some centuries, it became apparent that war was not really bloodthirsty enough to take the place of football. Besides, it was unfair to leave so many sociologists on the dole after they had gone to so much trouble to memorise the Offside Law, and the mating habits of the lesser spotted Stoke-on-Trent Skinhead.

Great Toilet Roll Decline

The other factors in the reversion from war to football were mainly economic. This refers, of course, to the crisis of supply and demand in the toilet roll industry. The toilet roll industry had existed for centuries as an offshoot from football; when a slack period arose with the close season the industry was able to scrape through on its sales to domestic users, before September again, and the renewed sales boom of a new season. Sales suffered, too, with the invention of the broken bottle; then much later on, with that triumph of hooligan technology, the sharpened steel comb. But the toilet roll industry was able to beat off each successive challenger with advances in its own technology; rocket-launched toilet rolls, self-propelled toilet rolls, and toilet rolls with built-in homing devices that 'fixed in' on the goalposts, and could not be intercepted before they had come to rest on the goalie's crossbar.

But with the long periods of war intervening, and the substitution of the toilet roll by the tank, a continuing decline set into the industry. Mills had to be closed down, workers laid off, and experimental laboratories shut down; whole areas of the country faced economic ruin as the once proud backbone of British industry and ingenuity met an incongruous end (*sic*).

Football Returns

After a time, things reached the stage where action had to be taken if this country was not to become a backward industrial power. So, by order of the Prime Minister, and grudging assent of the Committee of Pompous People in Charge of Football, war was stopped and football brought back. The move worked. Within months, the toilet roll industry was booming again, with similar happy stories in the broken bottle and sharpened steel comb industries. It was an unparalleled flush of success for the toilet roll industry, which was given recognition in the form of a thousand year contract to supply all the Football League Clubs' ends in the country.

Historians tell us that Man has evolved through several stages, including the toilet roll stage, to reach his present stage of development. First of all, he came out of the swamps. Man had to come ashore because it was very difficult to tell who was offside under water. Then he went through the Neolithic stage and then Neanderthal stage, before reaching the Sociologists' stage where everyone analysed everyone else, and told them they were confused. Now, scientists tell us, we are entering the Age of Football Man, the lowest form of civilisation Man has yet achieved.

Wherever archaeologists have discovered tablets of stone reporting the great events of the day—those early forerunners of our own beloved newspapers—they have found on turning the tablets over, a football page on the back. Prehistoric cave dwellers always reserved a section of their wall paintings for football match reports, and it is not at all uncommon to find prehistoric Skinheads' graffiti, such as "Cave End Skins Rule OK!" and "The Neolithic Mob are going to murder you lot next Saturday!" and "Fred Brontosaurus for England!"

Historians have charted its historical progress over the centuries, in frightened footnotes to history books :

> *It can truly be said that no age has been complete without its football, and assorted resultant barbarisms. (Although football tends to become suspended in time of war, as explained above, and also in time of things like the Great Plague when the carnage approaches that of the average Football Season, and there is no need for football as a population control mechanism, one of its many social functions.)*

Early cave paintings and religious paintings of religious ceremonies have revealed the existence of other integral parts of the game; many a cave painting contains etchings of Stone Age sociologists and Ice Age referees. Many a pot and pan, recovered from the ruins of some long forgotten Grandstand, carries symbols denoting the crowd's reaction to a referee disallowing a home team goal. Such symbols have existed throughout history, being handed down from father to son, and can still be found today on most football terraces on any Saturday afternoon. And excavations of hill-top Stone Age camps often reveal Stone Age referees tied to trees, with their hearts pierced by a Bovver Boot, as well as traces of the Skinheads' favourite pastime of that particular age—Brontosaurus Bashing.

Football Writers

Football has always been an inspiration to men of letters, and pen artists of all manner; particularly those inclined to write such things as "Burk Town Boot Boys Rule OK!" on walls and other public places. However, they are not alone in their endeavours; Shakespeare wrote about the game in *Macbeth*, which was one of the first hard-luck stories about a Scottish footballer who stabbed his Manager in a vain bid to get away and join the more lucrative pastures of English football. While Hamlet, of course, records the uncertainties of an early English Team Manager unable to decide whether or not to strangle his Goalkeeper for conceding an own goal in an important World Cup tie.

Even to this very day football continues to be a fascinating subject for Men of Letters too scared out of their wits ever to venture near a football ground, who, instead, remain at home writing books about it. I would like to state that this in no way applies to myself, who have been to more than 4½ Football League Grounds since my 10th birthday. Recent bestsellers on football include *Was God a Footballer?*; *A Clockwork Football*; *Live and Let Die*, the memoirs of a centre half; and *The Gory Game*, an in-depth investigation of football today.

It is necessary, at this early stage in the book, to explain that football is commonly referred to as "The Game", not to be confused with "Game, The" (see Handbook on Sex). The oldest profession must have existed even longer than football, because old prehistoric cave paintings also reveal the existence, at old prehistoric football matches, of footballers' groupies and other naked ladies of ill repute.

Since the dawn of history, since football existed in fact, sociologists have been telling us that football expresses deep atavistic urges among its fans. For instance, if you cannot have a Nuremberg rally, war or massacre, have a football match. This has not been clearly understood in football circles yet, since no one there knows what atavistic means.

Heroic Footballers

History has been full of great football men, and their actions have frequently changed the course of history, and sometimes, the interpretation of the Offside Law. For example, there was Napoleon, who took his entire first team squad to a World Cup match in Russia, but forgot to take enough steak to feed them and, as a consequence, they were heavily defeated. (NB: Footballers' favourite meal is steak, closely followed by steak, and it makes constant appearances throughout the history of The Game.)

Then there was Marco Polo, given a free transfer by Venice FC, who went on to make his name as a £200,000 centre forward for Peking Rovers. Another wanderer, Christopher Columbus, introduced football and steak to America.

(Historians dispute the reasons for the discovery of America; some think that Columbus, a travelling steak salesman, stumbled across it by accident, and thus was responsible for introducing the game there. Others subscribe to the "Clean-Up" theory, mentioned later on, whereby thousands of hard tackling centre halves were forced to cross the Atlantic because of a great refereeing purge taking place at the time. But others, after detailed study of old records and football programmes, say that it was a great talent-hunting expedition. Europe had run out of outside rights, and since Chinamen were too small, and rather boring, football managers decided to turn their attentions in the other direction.)

Of course, there was Henry VIII, who sacked six England Team Managers, before finding one who could build him a winning side. While further back, there was King Harold, who lost a crucial Cup Tie at Hastings, when he was blinded whilst going up to head a high ball.

History also tells of the world's first football hooligan, Genghis Khan. He told the magistrate that his mother did not love him, and that his father had always been nasty to him when he was a little boy. He got two years' probation. Football heroes from this century need no introduction; outstanding among these are Lloyd George and Winston Churchill, who led England to victory in the World Cups of 1914 and 1939 respectively. Both Finals against Germany went to extra time.

However, in spite of this fulsome pen picture of The Game spreading across the face of the earth, there are still wild, wild regions where the inhabitants are yet to hear of it. Every now and again, a group of nosy anthropologists discover a tribe of New Guinea headhunters who have never heard of football, and a trendy television crew head off in that direction, to record the Innocents, before football culture catches up with them, and mere head-hunters become reduced to Skinheads. (This, however, is against the normal run of things; most primitive jungle tribes are well acquainted with football, and its possibilities for multiple nasties, and have long since integrated it into their Initiation and Cannibalism Rites. The average twentieth-century Skinhead would not have much to learn from his head-hunting compatriots.)

Even On The Moon

Since football came to saturate the four corners of the earth, man has constantly been seeking to export it to the stars in manned space expeditions. One of the Earthman relics left on the Moon by the Americans when they first landed there, was a football, and a copy of the Rules of the Game. Some said that that was the best place for a copy of the Rules of the Game, since nobody took any notice of them down here. I think that is a very nasty and horrible thing to have said, and such nasty suggestions have no place in a dignified Handbook about Football such as this.

In addition to the manned landings on the Moon, and Man's efforts to stake out football pitches among the craters and volcanoes thereon, Russia and America have been active in dispatching unmanned expeditions to some of the far-off planets, particularly Jupiter, Mars and Neptune. Some of these are believed to have contained tough tackling centre halves, who were the despair of the Football Disciplinary Committees, the Red Cross of football, an obscure organisation which was brought into being as a sop to the public outcry about the butcherings on the world's football pitches. They are really a token body who content themselves with hanging the odd unpopular wing half when the public becomes disgusted at some of the more vicious antics of defenders.

However, these unmanned spacecraft are believed to contain autographed footballs for the benefit of any extra-terrestrial beings stupid enough to want to get involved with this planet's game. Also believed to be regularly placed on board, are several strips of playing kit, a pair of goalposts, a written explanation of the Offside Law, a pair of bovver boots, and some assorted typical items of fans' equipment such as rosettes, scarves and sawn-off shotguns. This was adjudged to be sufficient to give any alien being a broad outline of what football is about, and scare the wits out of him should he be contemplating visiting Earth.

One should also note at this point, the latest theories on the identity of Unidentified Flying Objects. It is believed in some circles

that UFO's are really extra terrestrial scouting missions by our inter-planetary cousins.

Indeed, radio receiving stations on Earth often report streams of radio signals from outer space, saying "I never done it!", "Who me, ref?", and "AAAAGGGGHH!", accompanied by the sound of studs tearing into flesh. All of which would seem to suggest that there are other Football Leagues active in this great Universe of ours.

Moon Transfers

Since earliest times, man has been fascinated by the prospect of football on other planets, by the prospect that there may be other intelligent beings behaving like ruthless savages playing football. Who has not thought at some time, when glancing up at the stars, those celestial floodlights, that there may be, out there in that great void, an intelligence, greater than our own, that understands the Offside Law?

These same people speculate that meteors and meteorites are really footballs from the solar systems of other planets, that have had an Almighty great boot from an Almighty little green centre half. You, on the other hand, may choose to think that such theories are potty, and disregard this section of the book altogether. Either way, most football clubs slip the odd fiver to their local observatory to keep an eye out for talent up there. No Manager can tolerate the thought that, somewhere out there, there may be a centre half who can kick harder than the one he has in his team already. And every Football League Manager in the country is looking forward to the day when he can play his first little green man in the first team. They reason that opposition defenders will be scared to tackle, for fear of catching some dreaded, unknown, alien disease that will be beyond the understanding of the club trainer when he runs on to the pitch to attend to injuries.

Clubs are attracted by the absence of gravity on the Moon, because they believe this means that their defenders would be able to kick opponents literally off the face of the Moon, and this is the reason for Britain's otherwise ludicrous interest in things celestial.

In fact, until this very day, football affords a great opportunity for study by the interested anthropologist; nowhere is Man to be found in such a primitive state, and no club is complete without its attached team of anthropologists doing a year's study on the behaviour of the first team squad, to get an insight into the behaviour patterns of apes.

The Pompous Committee

One cannot write about the origins of football without a further mention of the Committee of Pompous People in Charge of Football. There is nothing more calculated to bring a levity-laden chapter such as this, down to earth, than a detailed mention of this Committee. They have to be mentioned at this point because they think that they are too important to be left out of the second chapter of any book about football. And for the same reason, they insert themselves and their silly messages of goodwill, and sportsmanship, and all that, into the front of football programmes everywhere. And they also have to be mentioned at this stage because they often claim to have existed before football itself was invented. Few would dispute that claim.

The highest authorities in football are rarely seen by the general public. Some say this is because they are too wise to waste their perceptions upon the mass of the people. Others say this is because they labour long and hard over the welfare of The Game, and do not have the time to devote to empty publicity-making and popular phrase-making. Others still, say they are never seen in public because they are all asleep. And others, speculate that they may be dead, that they may never even have existed in the first place, that football is a natural phenomenon, handed down from father to son, since the dawn of creation and the Offside Law, and has never needed a guiding hand from the Committee of Pompous People in Charge of Football, or anyone else.

What is certain, is that the People in Charge of Football always have a spokesman for their point of view when anyone suggests that it is time for a change of any sort in The Game.

Their Spokesman

A. J. R. Thingame is the bumbling spokesman for the Committee of Pompous People in Charge of Football, who is wheeled out to press and television twice a year to denounce the latest, horrific, progressive, proposals afoot in football, such as turning grounds into community centres and paying apprentices more than their present 30p a week. Other onerous duties of the Committee spokesman include putting out press statements twice a year denouncing all horrific, progressive ideas afloat in the press at that time, and a yearly appearance at the Annual General Meeting of Pompous People in Charge of Football, attended by most Chairmen, Directors, and Unelected Very Important Officials, to denounce all the advanced ideas that have been circulated in football that year.

It is at such meetings that A. J. R. Thingame delivers his thunderous lines: "If God had wanted footballers to have been paid appearance bonuses, he would have made it so". "I have never heard so much rubbish in my life." "If God had wanted English teams to play in Europe, he would have left Europe attached to England instead of casting it off on its own—a just punishment for stealing our national game.

The Annual General Meeting of the Committee of Pompous People in Charge of Football, is known in the Game as the Old Boys' Groan-In, when the dithering ancients who run our national game spend a fortnight every year drinking each other's brandy, bought on the proceeds of those of us who have to enter football grounds through the turnstiles every week, lashing out at all the progressive ideas put forward in football over the previous year, attacking the behaviour of crowds going to football matches, attacking the people who do not go to football matches, the players, the press, and everyone outside football and in modern life today, except equally Pompous Committees like themselves, lamenting the lack of discipline in the modern game, and the lack of self-discipline in modern society.

CHAPTER THREE

The Team

Great Free Wallchart Offer!!

Free of charge to all readers of The Football Handbook
To End All Football Handbooks. *This superb Colour
Wallchart of the Ham United team. And so you can keep
up to date with the action right through the season, we are
also providing, free of charge, with the Chart, a black felt
tip pen with which you can cross off any limbs that get
broken in the course of the season, or any players who
get transferred or mutilated. Keep up to date with the
stars! Just send a postal order for £40, to Crackalimb
Limited, The Casualty Ward, Bloodsquirt Hospital, Blood
Park, Near Ham United Football Ground.*

A Typical Team

Ham United are a typical English football team. In other words,
a bunch of stars, superstars, tenacious defenders, ball artists,
cloggers, pansies, con-men, illiterate Scots, home-loving, hard-
drinking, wife-swapping professional footballers.

There is Vincent, the crooning, moody, sensitive superstar, who
has a boutique for every day of the season, and who is usually
too temperamental to play football come Saturday afternoon.

There is Mugsy, the team 'chopper' who does the nasties to
the opposition; generally regarded as the nastiest thing outside the
Chamber of Horrors. There is Brains, the intelligent member of
the team, who is kept on for the purpose of talking to press and
television commentators.

One of the few talented footballers in the team is Barclay, the
team's coloured player, whom no one dare throw out of the team,
however badly he plays, because he would take the club before the
Race Relations Board.

The team's youngster is Davy, a naive 18-year-old who has just
broken through to the first team from the youth team, and who still
thinks football is all it is made out to be. He missed the last home

game because he spilled egg all down his nice new jumper, so his mummy would not let him go out and play football.

Then there is the Captain, Robby Score, OBE, Queen's Award to Industry, blond, curly-haired housewives' heartthrob, on loan from 'Roy of the Rovers' comic strip. He can do no wrong. (He cannot play football either, but that is beside the point.)

All these and more, are presided over by Ringmaster in Chief, Manager Jock McNivers, hard-talking, no-nonsense, fire-eating Celt who addresses the players through an interpreter.

However, enough of these flourishes of the pen. Football clubs' programmes always carry detailed analytical breakdowns of the lives, loves and careers of the combatant teams. Why should match-day spectators be the only ones to suffer these boring analyses of boring people? Here, for the stupefaction of all mugs who have bought *The Football Handbook To End All Football Handbooks*, is the complete analysis of the eleven stars, superstars, tenacious defenders, ball artists, cloggers, pansies, con-men, illiterate Scots, home-loving, hard-drinking, wife-swapping sadists that make up that household name, Ham United.

Goalkeeper	1 Fingers	Fingers played 261 games for Dartmoor FC, before earning full remission and transferring to Pentonville Wanderers. We do not know how he got here.
Right Back	2 Sid Scythe	The scything tackle is named after him. He reckons to break two opponents' legs in every match, and is heartbroken if he has not had the opposing winger over in the first three minutes.
Left Back	3 Jock Maul	Fierce, whisky drinking, tartan-haired Scot who trains on his oats and drinks his own specially brewed brand of malt whisky. Jock Maul pollutes his side off the field with so many whisky fumes that opposing wingers are knocked out long before they reach him. And if they do reach him, they are certainly knocked out.
Right Half	4 Masher	Masher arrived at the club one Saturday morning, and no one really had the nerve to ask him to leave. Masher is 22 stone, and 6 ft. wide.

Centre Half	5 Mugsy	The team's chopper; the one what does the nasties to the opposition, and sometimes to his own side, when he gets carried away. But it is normally his opponents who get carried away, on a stretcher. "The thickest thing to have ever worn studs," is how his Manager describes him when out of earshot.
Left Half	6 Robby Score	Blond and curly-haired Captain, housewives' heart-throb on loan from 'Roy of the Rovers' comic strip. He can do no wrong (he can't play football either, but that is irrelevant). The face that launched a million detergent packets.
Outside Right	7 Paddy O'Guinness	The best friend of every publican in London. Discovered by a Ham United scout, while playing for the Wimpey Works team, Shovel FC.
Inside Right	8 Brains	The intelligent member of the team, rumoured to have an IQ of over 30. He is the one who reads the team sheet to the rest of the lads on Saturday morning, to tell them which of them is playing.
Centre Forward	9 Vincent	This is the flash one, the club superstar; the crooning (he has cut six records), moody, sensitive genius who has a boutique for every match of the season, and who is usually too temperamental to play football come Saturday afternoon. Rumoured to wear a pink jock-strap. Vincent is having a £250,000 super-pad built in the Kent countryside with his own private football ground built in, so that he can continue, at close quarters, his coaching of the local girls' team—Scrubbers XI.

Inside Left	10 **Davy**	Nice, young 18-year-old lad who still thinks the girls hanging around outside the changing rooms after every home game are looking for autographs. The only member of the team who still lives at home. Missed the last home game because he spilled egg all down his nice new jumper, and so his mummy would not let him go out and play football. Still has pictures of footballers on his bedroom walls.
Outside Left	11 **Barclay**	Tall, lanky, skilful West Indian, whom no one dare throw out of the team, however badly he plays, because he always threatens to report them to the Race Relations Board.

The thickest member of the team is made Captain, unless a 'Roy of the Rovers' type is available.

Reunion at the start of the season is always a happy time at a football club. The players are introduced to any new player signed in the close season. The players whose positions in the team are threatened by any new arrival, quietly take him behind the nearest bushes and, while the Manager is not looking, asphyxiate him. However, no such problems arose at the beginning of this season since Mr. McNivers had not bought anyone during his time at the club, because all the forwards had played well the previous season, and dropping any of the defenders would lead to all sorts of complications like having his face smashed in.

There are, of course, many other players on the club's books, mainly promising youngsters who hope to follow Davy's example, and aged veterans, whom successive Managers have tried to chase out of the woodwork, but who keep cropping up at the back of the team as they run out on to the pitch. More about them later. They are too trivial to be dealt with alongside our worthy heroes outlined here.

Suspension

This leaves 27 players missing from the line-up because they are suspended. One of the rules of football most commonly called into usage, is the suspension of players. Any player receiving three bookings in one season for various nasties on the pitch, is automatically suspended for three games. This means that the player can join in all the normal club activities like training, wife-swapping, and picking up Bunny Girls, but is forbidden to play in any actual football game, whether league or cup. In the wider context of footballers' life styles, this may not seem to be a very great loss. Managers like to keep a tight rein on their suspended players, and also keep them in touch with the latest clogging techniques, for when they are brought back into the game. A club's suspended players are nearly always ordered by the Manager to watch all games they are suspended from, so for this purpose, most clubs have a specially reserved section of the stand for suspended players to crowd into. This way, it is felt, they won't forget what football is all about during their enforced retirement.

Landladies

One cannot introduce the team without a brief mention of that stalwart of English football teams, the footballer's long-suffering landlady. Most club Managers like to install their players in quiet bed and breakfast digs well away from the centre of town, and the myriad temptations of drink, gambling, Bunny Girls and naked ladies of ill repute. That is the start of much trouble for these beleaguered matrons. (Not that they let their guests get away with much; many a hard tackling sadist wilts at the sound of his

landlady's voice, and cowers at the foot of the stairs when she bawls him out for walking on the carpet in his muddy boots.)

Most footballers end up devising various means of escape for a night on the town with the boys. Mugsy has a chute from his window to a waiting transit van. When Vincent lived in digs (before the club allowed him to move to his super pad in the countryside, where he could coach his favourite girls' football team in seclusion for ever) he kept a rope hanging from his window to the door of his waiting Aston Martin.

The wise footballer's landlady keeps a shotgun stashed away in the cupboard for disciplinary purposes. Apart from her ability to handle the gun, the main requirement from a landlady is to be willing to have one of her rooms converted to a deep freeze, big enough to contain enough steak for a footballer for a week.

Landladies compete for the better members of the team, although all types have their advantages. Living at home with tough, tackling defenders is never much fun, because they are for ever tripping you up, even when you bring them their steak and cup of tea in the morning. Living with superstars means you have lots of little girls coming to the door all the time asking for their autographs, and lots of big girls coming to the door asking for something else altogether. Silly little boys peer in through the windows, and are for ever writing rude words on the nice new sports cars parked outside. To overcome these problems, liberated landladies work to a rota and take it in turns to have the club superstar, chopper, hard worker, and the rest.

The Manager

The most important member of any team is its Manager. Jock McNivers is one of the great characters of English football, and one of the many Scots in the English game. He got his present job, from a short list of 28, by his fiery behaviour in his interview with the Board. His tough, rasping Scots accent so impressed the Board that, although they had not understood a word he said, they thought here, at long last, was the man who would put Ham United back into shape, on the path to victory, and away from the path to drink, wife-swapping, gambling, and naked ladies of ill repute.

The Board were not worried about not understanding what the man had been saying, since the players were pretty dumb anyway, and would recognise sufficient aggression in his manner, to get on with the job and stop mucking around.

Language has never been a problem to Jock. Before he was Manager of Ham United, he coached the well-known Greek team, Patratriokoas Carapanaioas, a team of sleazy, untrustworthy dagoes from an obscure mountain top in Central Greece. After screaming at them in his broad Scots dialect for two weeks, he managed to raise them from their customary stupor to move the ball around for 10 out of the 90 minutes in every game. As this was ten minutes more than any other team of sleazy, untrustworthy dagoes were playing, they won the Greek League, and Jock hastily added this to the string of accomplishments on his headed notepaper, preparatory to his claim for a job in the English Football League. His honours list as a Manager already included a string of outstanding League victories with remote croft sides in the central highlands of Scotland, and the Armenian Girls' Boys Brigade Youth XI.

Jock was brought in to manage Ham United after the Club had had a particularly lean spell over several seasons. The team had been scoring goals all right, but they had been conceding a great many, and were forgetting their priorities. This was sacrilege to the Directors, those learned men of football, who suspected that the team were forgetting that modern football is about stopping the other side scoring, and not actually scoring yourself.

McNivers was viewed as a typical member of the new, tough breed of no-nonsense Manager coming into the game at that time, and thus just the sort of man to pull the team into shape. And the way he set about his task at Ham United left nobody under any illusions as to how he was intending to run things.

Fines For Scoring

I spoke to him after he had been at the club for a week. "Yes, I am well pleased. I am more pleased that we have not lost any games, than that we have won any, of course. This goals nonsense has gone on far too long; it is high time people in the game took a stand against it. It is a menace that has got to be stamped out, and I would like to say here and now that I am all in favour of the new, increased penalties for anyone scoring, or attempting to score, a goal. I think the suggestion of a moat around the penalty area is a bit drastic, but we may yet be forced to do that if this wave of goal scoring cannot be curbed."

On his arrival, McNivers immediately doubled the number of training sessions, and imposed a fine of £50 on anyone seen entering the opponent's half of the field during a game.

"I saw the light in Greece," he told me in a break from extra training. "Anyone showing the least amount of skill in a training session was fined £10 and sent straight home. It's not quite the same here, yet. Old habits die hard and several of the players still think it is better to score than not to score. But we are working on this, and I am hopeful that we shall come up with something soon."

How are the players responding to the new concept of football at Ham United? I spoke to centre forward, national heart-throb 'The Face that Wet a Thousand Knickers' and England star, Vincent Spooner. Did he feel that the new tactics were detrimental to his style of play?

"Come again?" was his immediate reply. But after thought, he read a prepared statement, pressed into his hands by tough, new breed of Manager, no-nonsense Jock McNivers, who was muttering under his breath, "If English football is full of raving little poofdas, like this one, I'm going back to Greece".

In a halting voice, Vincent read for the benefit of all the assembled pressmen; "I have complete confidence in the management of tough, no-nonsense, new breed of Manager, Jock McNivers. I think what he is doing is the right thing for football, and for Ham United, and I want to say how all the lads here at Blood Park are right behind him in everything he does. I am deeply sorry for my mistakes in the past: I know I have gone a bit wild on a few occasions, and have even been known to score several hat-tricks for the team. But I have promised the new Manager that I will watch my behaviour very carefully in future, and do my best to fit into his plans".

For the comments of a relative newcomer to the game, I spoke to lanky, former England Schoolboys' Captain, and top of his class at the grammar school, Davy Trusty.

"I think it is a good thing," he told me. "I scored four goals last season, and the new boss has set me a target of two by the end of this season. I think it is a very good idea, and I have promised the new boss full effort throughout the season in order to try and reach my target."

The effect of McNivers' new measures are already being felt off the field, as well as on. At least one player who had previously requested a transfer has now withdrawn his request. Brains, the man behind the midfield of Ham United, and who is renowned throughout the football world for his ability to complete the *Daily Splurge* Junior Crossword in less than 90 minutes, told me that his talk with the new Manager had convinced him that his future would be best spent at Ham United, after all.

"It was either that, or a free transfer to Aberdeen Albion," Brains muttered, as he emerged stony faced from the office of tough-talking, no-nonsense, new-breed of Manager Jock McNivers, who could be heard in the background, pounding his desk, and shouting, "How dare you come in here snivelling for a transfer".

For a final word on Ham United's prospects under the new system I returned to tough-talking, no-nonsense, new breed of Manager, Jock McNivers. "I think it will work out," he told me. "The key word is 'workrate'. We have to improve our workrate enormously, we have to get far more professional. In our away match at Muggingthorpe last week, I caught several of the players taking a break half way through the match and going off and eating oranges. It won't do. I fined them all £25, and told them to report for extra training the next day. This is not a holiday camp, you know. I have told the players that scoring goals is not what it is about in my type of football. That sort of nonsense is right out. Any player scoring two or more goals in any match must submit his reason in writing to me within 21 days, and then, after three offences, he is out of the game for six weeks, banned. I am going to put steel into this club if it kills me."

Public Opinion

For the opinion of the man in the street, I stopped to talk to Mickey Menace, the well-known local soccer hooligan and all round thug. After first offering me some aggro, which I courteously declined, Mr. Menace settled down to talk about the changes in the club he has supported since birth. (He was, in fact, born under the Skull End, in a goalless draw against Muggingthorpe Town, 22 years ago.)

"I think it is a good thing, moosh," he told me, twirling a rusty iron bar in one hand, and sensually fondling a bicycle chain in the other.

"Me and me mates, see, we come here for a fight, a lark and a bit of the other in the back of the stand, and we keep getting interrupted by this goals nonsense. Well, I mean, it ain't right, is it? So I reckon this McNivers geezer has got the right idea. Give it to 'em in the knackers. No messing about, straight up the floozy. Know what I mean? Now where's me fee?"

The McNivers plan paid quick dividends. The club won all their home games 1–0, and drew all their away games 0–0, thus coming top of Division I by a record margin, entitling the club to play in Europe the following season. And that is something the new Manager is looking forward to avidly; "We're going to teach those damn foreigners a thing or two!" McNivers told me through an interpreter.

Agents

One cannot talk about football teams without mentioning that other equally important group of people in the game, their agents. Most of the Ham United players' businesses are handled by Harry Sharp, Consolidated Conmen Ltd., of Lewisham and Soho. This is just one of the many dedicated football fans who offer their services to the game free of charge, at a very reasonable rate. Such men are to be found in all Football League clubs, only too willing to place their services at the disposal of anyone stupid enough to take them up on anything. Consolidated Conmen, in particular, are men who are renowned for having the interests of the professional footballer at heart.

When I first interviewed Harry Sharp about his work, he told me, "Personally, I would abolish the football aspect of it altogether".

This morning, Davy has an appointment with nice Mr. Screw of the Ron E. Dubious Organisation, yet another setup dedicated to the welfare of aspiring young footballers, particularly when it looks as if they are going to make a packet.

Sidelines

The opening of shops, boutiques and showrooms, is now an everyday part of the average footballer's life. So, too, is the process

2—FH *

of giving your name to various products, whether in fact you use them or not. It is Jock's ambition to give his name to a brand of whisky; while Paddy is believed to have had a brewery named after him somewhere in the South of Ireland. The same place is also believed to extend a permanent open invitation to Ireland's favourite son to sample the beer produced therein, free of charge. So every summer holiday, Paddy packs his wife and kids into his ageing car, and sets off in search of this private Nirvana. He always ends up getting hopelessly lost before he has got anywhere near the place.

Roddy, as captain and international player of great renown, has all sorts of things named after him, and dedicated to him. You can buy the perfume, allegedly worn by Robby's wife, the former nun and Bunny Girl, Priscilla Score. Then there are Robby Score weed killer, peppermints, toilet rolls, after-shave, chocolate, washing-up liquid, sportswear, nail varnish, all of these products allegedly being used by Roddy in his everyday life.

To keep up with the amount of sponsorship Robby is expected to be involved in, he has to set aside at least one day of his week entirely to photo shots and publicity sessions for his many endorsements. Hardly a day goes by without his being photographed cleaning his teeth, chewing toffees, driving his car, and pulling on his Robby Score sportswear football kit. But whether Robby's endorsement really has the desired effect, remains to be seen. For every mum who lovingly runs out and buys a packet of Robby Score toothpaste, there is an infuriated Muggingthorpe or Blimp Town supporter who runs amok in his local supermarket at the sight of so many Ham United endorsed products.

Agents find difficulty in finding products for Brains to endorse; his is a difficult image. Even the experienced hands of Consolidated Conmen of Lewisham and Soho have been unable to cope with the image of an intelligent footballer. Harry Sharp, king of the Cons, gave up in despair after two weeks when Brains actually wanted to know whether the toothpaste he was extolling *was* "The Mostest on the Market".

Earlier in his career, in fact, Brains achieved legendary proportions in football as the only footballer ever to actually write his own newspaper column in the papers. The experiment only lasted three weeks, before Fleet Street hack reporters rose up in arms to complain that this was a flagrant use of non-union scab labour to perform a function that was normally and perfectly easily performed by journalists. It was unfair, they claimed, to use skilled labour in a job that was traditionally the prerogative of unskilled hack journalists. Who did this upstart think he was? This was called the Intelligent Footballer Strike.

Agents are also confused when they try to find products for Davy to lend his name to. He has a nice image, and this is something totally outside the normal comprehension of the footballers' agent.

A Football Ghost

No footballer is complete without his ghosted column in the newspapers. Nearly all the Ham United players have columns somewhere in some sort of paper. Fingers is the star name in *Inside*, the weekly newspaper by and for Dartmoor inmates. While Jock appears every week in the *Aberdeen Argosy*, and can be found on the pages of most Scots newspapers, extolling the virtues of Scotland's leading export, Robby appears twice weekly in the *Daily Clarion*, in the "Wonderful, Wonderful World of Robby Score". Vincent, Barclay and Robby also appear in innummerable girls' magazines. Here, they are expected to give their columns over to answering silly questions from silly girls.

For example, here are these silly questions from a typical week in girls' magazines. To Robby: "Is your hair naturally ginger, or did you dye it?" and "Don't you think it would be better with green streaks?" (To Barclay: "What is your favourite meal?")

Personal Appearances

All players at some time or other in their careers, have to open shops, showrooms and establishments of various kinds. The players spend weeks beforehand practising their lines.

Thus, Robby, opening a sex bookshop in Acton: "I would just like to say how very pleased I am to open this 'ere Sexerama Bookshop. Sex is definitely 'ere to stay; after all, sex is everywhere, isn't it? It's in the dressing rooms at the ground, it's on the pitch, and even our great Manager says you can't beat sex."

After a round of applause from the assembled mums and dads and ogling 13-year-old schoolgirls who have played truant from school to see him, Robby spends ten minutes signing autographs, including plaster casts, boots, broken milk bottles, sharpened steel combs, knickers (sometimes with the owner still wearing them) and last week's photo from the *Daily Bugle*, a two-page spread of Robby in the nude. He then moves on to open a Chinese restaurant in Surbiton. For this, some hasty speech re-writing is required, and Harry sets to, in the back of Robby's Rolls Royce, while Robby devotes his attentions to a nice young lady who asked if Robby would give her some personal tuition on the lesser known aspects of the Offside Law.

At Surbiton, his speech reads : "I would just like to say how very pleased I am to open this 'ere Chinese restaurant. I think Chinese is definitely 'ere to stay. After all, Chinese is everywhere, isn't it? It's in the dressing room at the ground, it's on the pitch, and our great Manager says that you can't beat a good Chinese." From here, the whizz kid is whizzed on to a pea-processing plant, deep in the Kent countryside.

Here, before a crowd of 15 yokels, 27 photographers, 42 reporters, 17 social workers doing a study of the life-style of workers in a pea processing plant, the village policeman and lots of silly little boys who just want Robby's autograph, Robby delivers his revised speech.

"I would just like to say how very pleased I am to come 'ere today, and open this peas factory. I think peas is definitely 'ere to stay. After all, peas is everywhere, ain't they? Be reasonable. They're in the dressing room at the club, in the shop around the corner, and on the pitch. Even our great Manager, Mr. McNivers, says you can't beat a good pea."

To complete his day, Robby is rushed by helicopter to Harlow, where he is due to open a gas showroom.

One of the things to bear in mind about footballers' public utterances, apart from the fact that they are totally devoid of any intelligent thinking, is that they never dare say anything bad about their Manager. In fact, they take every opportunity to offer up unsolicited words of praise to the Great Man, whose hand can erase them from the team-sheet at a stroke.

Fan Mail

All clubs receive a never-ending stream of letters asking the players for autographs, giving words of advice on the tactics, and inviting the players to attend parties thrown by naked ladies of ill repute. All clubs take care to censor players' incoming mail, to protect them from the temptations and pitfalls of the outside world. Ham United are no exception, and Chairman Knowlesworth-Blair has his personal secretary and masseuse, Miss Suzy Goodtime, in-spect all players' mail, and pass on to him all correspondence from naked ladies of ill repute.

Young girls write in asking for locks of Vincent's hair, or signed photos of him in the bath. Mums write in to Robby Score, asking for his autograph, and enclosing recipes for Davy, "Because he looks so thin, and I'm sure he does not get a proper meal".

Mums and other nice sorts of people, of whom there are believed to be 215 left in football, also write in to Robby begging him to tell them that he did not tell the nasty man from the television company to "bugger off" the other day, as the man in the news-paper had reported. Fingers tends to get letters from old cell mates, who are still inside, asking for tickets for the next home game.

Mugsy's Memoirs

I conclude this chapter with a brief study of the background of one of the average members of Ham United Club—Mugsy, their centre half. Only later did I discover that I was the first reporter to interview Mugsy and get back alive.

I spoke to Mugsy in his book-lined study, which was specially installed by his landlady next to the garage she had converted into a deep freeze for his steak.

"I don't read none of them," Mugsy assured me with a wave of the hand towards the tiers of classical works that lined the room. "It's the boss. He always tells you to have a book-lined study built into your place for when geezers like you come along to do the old interviews, like, you know what I mean?"

I said I sympathised.

"It's a £30 fine if he sees me talking on the tele, and he sees it's in the living room or the backyard."

Having then actually sat down to start the interview proper, we found that we had not actually said anything to each other after 90 minutes, so Mugsy broke the session up by saying, "Wait here a minute, I've got something that will interest you". I sat rooted to my chair in terrified anticipation.

After a couple of minutes, he returned with his lovingly cared for collection of steel-rimmed left boots with which he has maimed opponents on the four corners of the earth. After I had politely examined the endless display of blood-stained boots, he showed me another of his treasured possessions; the scrapbook in which he keeps all his newspaper cuttings from when he is booked or sent off by referees.

"Look here," said Mugsy pointing to a particularly grubby ancient photo. "This was the very first time I was sent off. I was $7\frac{1}{2}$ at the time." In front of me was a faded picture of a wee lad, almost drowned in his own shorts, standing on his opponent's head, and scowling at the referee. "I done him before kick-off, that was me mistake," Mugsy explained.

It took Mugsy some time to learn from such mistakes. At $9\frac{1}{2}$ he was made captain of his School team, because he was by far the biggest and nastiest bully boy in the school, and no one else really fancied the job of ordering Mugsy about on the pitch. But Mugsy's spell as captain was short lived. Every time he came up to the centre circle to shake hands with the referee and the opposing side's captain, at the start of a match, he went in hard on both of them, before the clean, crisp, white schoolboy size football had moved from the centre spot. He was inevitably ordered off by prostrate referees, in this situation.

For Mugsy, it was a hard life; the sort of life that was later to make him a man feared by other men. He got off to a good start, of course, by being a boy feared by other boys. Mugsy, as all professional footballers invariably are, was something of a failure in the classroom. In fact, he was a dunce. When he was not sitting at the back, throwing toilet rolls at his hapless teachers, he spent his lessons sitting at the lathe in the metalwork shop, sharpening his studs, and blunting the toecap of his boots, in eager anticipation of the next school game.

Invariably, too, his teachers gave Mugsy up, and he was constantly being told to stand outside in the corridor. There is no telling how Mugsy would have fared with modern teaching methods, which would have had his teacher giving in to all of his little harmless whims, and letting him do his own thing.

But, once out in the corridors of the school, Mugsy soon got bored, being too thick to count the dots on the wallpaper, or make patterns out of the coloured tiles on the floor. Such boredom was anathema to a person of Mugsy's vivid imagination and vibrant intellect. After a couple of minutes he would wander off around the school, one-handedly picking up other boys who had been thrown out of the class for disobedience, and bouncing them first off the wall, and then off the ceiling.

When he got bored with this, which was generally not for three or four hours because he found it great fun, Mugsy would go off and smash a few tables and chairs before ambling off to the local amateur football ground, where he would see his heroes in action, deep in their training for the day. This was the part of the day Mugsy loved best; here at last were real men, heroes he could identify with. No going and standing in the corridor if you hit somebody in this game, or if you weren't top of the class.

As Mugsy watched the first team players kick and generally savage reserve team players in a practice game, he said to himself, slowly, "That's for me". An idea had been planted, unwittingly, in the lad's boots (he did not have a brain to have anything planted in) that was to wreak havoc across Europe in the years to come.

Mugsy learnt much from watching the local teams like this. His mother would come and watch him in school games, when he was not suspended, and shout and yell encouragement from the touchline: "Kill 'im! Get 'im in the goolies! Break 'is leg!" And she would throw Mugsy a sweetie every time he chopped somebody. This was to be Mugsy's first incentive bonus.

Fingers spends his spare time coaching the local prison team. Jock and Paddy spend their spare time coaching their respective pub sides.

Great Competition!! To obtain your Mugsy punchbag and eight dustcovers of The Football Handbook To End All Football Handbooks, *and a bloodstained limb from each of the last four opponents you have played against, to: Honest Vince, The Flat Above The Secondhand Car Showrooms, Dubious Street, Lewisham.*

The Club

Get your Free *Ham United fixture list at the unbelievable bargain price of 90p! FROM: Charlie Swindle & Sons, Unilateral Scrapyards, Off Sales Dept., Hackney, London. And we promise you that this time they are this year's fixtures! And if they are not, and we again accidentally send all our customers the previous season's fixtures, like we did last year, well a bit of nostalgia never hurt anyone did it? It certainly never hurt people like us! To get the most out of your football, let Uncle Charlie get the most out of you!!!*

The Big Happy Family

The easiest way to understand the structure of a football club is to envisage it as one big happy family. At the head of the family are the wise parents, who control the pocket money, and know it all. These are the Directors. Then, if it is a very posh family, there is the nanny, employed by the parents to control the children, and stop them pestering mummy and daddy, and who can be sacked at two seconds' notice by mummy and daddy. This is the Manager. Then there are the little children, scampering around in blissful ignorance, who have no real say in the family at all. These are the footballers.

The All-Important Chairman

Let us start our analysis at the top. The most important person in any football club is the Chairman, and this is certainly the case with Ham United. The Chairman of Ham United Football Club is Sir Derek James Arthur Knowlesworth-Blair, KBE. Sir Derek wishes it to be made known that he thinks he is so important that he should not be described on the same page as his fellow directors, who follow in the next paragraph. The description of Chairman

Knowlesworth-Blair is therefore suspended from this page, and from the next six matches, and fined £50.

The Board of Directors are a group of men selected for the job because of their deep seated and life-long devotion to football, who just happen to have pots of money as well.

The Aged Millionaire

There is Sir Brian Hethlewaite Thwaites, 87, retired multi-millionaire. Sir Brian retired at the age of 70, and then planned to sojourn to Hove, to spend the rest of his life in abject misery, along with his life-long savings of £467,000,000.34p. But his Rolls Royce got caught up in the crowds at Ham United's home game against Brute FC, and when the club officials discovered his great wealth, they persuaded him that he had in fact arrived at Hove. And so, at every home game, his bath chair is wheeled out to the pitch, and he is parked on the touchline, and the Club Secretary whispers in his ear that he is really watching Hove's summer beach festivities.

The Rev.

Also on the Board is the Reverend James Carleworth Bore. He is not a money man, but is thought to have exceptionally good connections through his job. ("We like to think we have friends in all the right places," Chairman Knowlesworth-Blair.) One of the many advantages of having a good Reverend on the Board, is that he can be wheeled out to the press, when the team has had an extraordinarily lucky victory, and says things like, "The Good Lord saw fit to bestow two full points on us today, and who are we to question his judgment?"

To which there is really no answer. And again, such things as, "We like to keep our lines to the Lord clear at all times", after the ball has been cleared off the Ham United goal line seven times in one match. The Chairman regards the Reverend as his secret weapon against Claytown (Ham United's deadliest rivals).

One of the wiliest members of the Board is Daniel Smith-Jones, an up-and-coming slave plantation owner. He deals with the mortgages that fans take out on their fan gear. It was his wily idea that stopped the slump in Ham United's home attendances last year—to rope in passers-by who were stopping off to buy Hot Dogs outside the ground, Smith-Jones ordered that onions and tomato sauce be served only inside the ground.

How They Chose The Directors

The process of appointing a director is a long and arduous one. ("The Team is selected, the Manager is chosen, Directors are appointed, I was anointed," Chairman Knowlesworth-Blair). The traditional method is to find a family with low intelligence and lots of money, and simply appoint all the directors from there. It is thought that directorship, like all the best business matters, is best dealt with on a family level. This method, however, has complications; every time the family in question sits down to breakfast, it is a board meeting, and if the toast is burnt the Manager can get sacked.

Ham United, as the Chairman never ceases to tell over-awed foreign visitors, are one of the go-ahead clubs using the most modern methods of director selection. With the help of Director Smith-Jones' personal pocket computer, with which he keeps track of the work rate of his employees in his various scattered slave plantations, the Board cross reference *Who's Who*, the membership list of the Bags of Money Club, St. James's, Whitehall, and the list of the 2,131 people in Britain known to have never attended a football match. This is thought to produce the right mixture of pomposity, ignorance and money thought to be necessary to produce a good Football Club Director.

Any names appearing on all three lists are automatically short-listed. Candidates on the short list are then put through a Sociability test—this involves their being shut in the same room as a FOOTBALLER. If, after 70 minutes, nothing has been said, the candidate is adjudged to be of director material.

Vital Questions

This is followed by the financial test, the most important test of all. This involves the answering of two questions:

(1) A player appeals to the Board for more money, because his mortgage is running into difficulties, and his wife is expecting her third baby. Do you answer "YES, certainly you can have some more". Or do you answer "NO, the club cannot possibly afford to meet your demands. We are already deep in the red"?

(2) The Chairman comes to you and asks for £200,000 for ground improvements, that is to re-stock the Directors' Bar. Do you answer "NO, the club cannot possibly afford it, we are already deeply in debt"? Or do you answer "YES, certainly! Here, let me give you a cheque"?

If your answers are "NO" to (1) and "YES" to (2), you have passed the final test, and are now a director of Ham United. As such, you are entitled to the free use of he Directors' Bar, personal aeroplane, and all directors' groupies. It is already taken for granted that you smoke big, fat cigars, drink double-whiskys, which you order in a loud, boorish voice, sneer at your inferiors, consider everyone apart from your fellow directors to be your inferior, and own a big, flash car which you will instinctively park outside the players' entrance to the ground, to remind them who is boss at this club.

The Programme

Some people say that one of the reasons people like to become directors is because they get their name printed very prominently at the front of the club's match-day programme. I am sure this is not true.

The club programme, apart from being a virtual handbill for the Chairman's firm and its products, is an extremely interesting piece of literature, and indirectly tells us much about the game as a whole. At least that's what sociologists say. Club programmes invariably contain glowing introductions to the day's referee, sometimes printing his address, as a subtle warning of what may happen if he does not co-operate with the home team. Other references are more subtle; "Referee Bloggs lives within brick throwing distance of the Skull End", is regarded as sufficient to remind the hapless fellow of his priorities.

The Editor

Last week's match is always reviewed in the programme, in length, or with the utmost brevity, depending on the result. Sometimes this particular part of the programme exercises the wits of the programme editor to the fullest extent. The programme at Ham

United is written, edited and printed by elderly Arthur Squib, a tame hack journalist who also edits *Knowlesworth News*, the trade paper of the Knowlesworth Organisation. Not surprisingly, the programme is full of adverts for Knowlesworth trusses and pogo sticks. Arthur also does the photographs for the programme, although strangely, he never seems to manage to take a photograph when the opposition is scoring a goal.

When Ham United hit a lean spell in their scoring, the time is adjudged right for packing the programme with endless reminiscences of Ham United's Golden Years, widely believed to have been in the early 1900's, and thus, just beyond the pale of living memory.

Such phrases as "The team was involved in an eight-goal thriller" mean they got hammered 8–0. Home defeats present a real problem; for then, everybody has witnessed the debacle, and some ingenuity is required to explain it all away. Here, Arthur is permitted : "The team had an off day", while he can use "The team was not at full strength". After that any deviating from the party line—that Ham United and Knowlesworth trusses and pogo sticks can do no wrong—places him in utter jeopardy. Once his allowance of explanations has run out, very heavy home defeats are buried away in long-winded explanations of why the visiting team wore an all-white strip this time, what the weather was like, and didn't the Chairman's wife look lovely in her new pink hat, and would the Skull End please stop doing multiple nasties to visiting supporters, because it gets so embarrassing for the Board to have to explain to visiting directors?

The Teams Are Always Winning Something

To preserve club morale when the team is not doing well, clubs have lots of reserve teams which are entered for various meaningless reserve competitions with other clubs' reserve teams. This means that *someone* in the club is *bound* to be winning *something* at any one time.

There are Second Team Leagues and Cups, Youth Team Leagues, and Cups, etc. etc. Also, all the clubs' teams make separate tours abroad, competing for sundry foreign trophies with sundry foreigners. Ham United retain an extraordinary number of these reserve sides—far more than there are competitions in fact. The reserve under-18 youth side is believed to pass its time with spear throwing and underarm tiddlywinks contests. However, with this system, hardly a week goes by without Ham United winning a trophy of some sort.

The inside cover of the club's programme for first team games, where not carrying the names of the club's directors, is chocabloc with Ham United's honours list. Starting with their famous League victories in 1917, 1908, 1857 and 1641—the latter unverified, but Chairman Knowlesworth-Blair assured me that he had come across it in his family archives.

Dubious Honours

Some of the other honours further down the list are a bit more dubious. The All-Panamanian Soccer Challenge Cup, won on the team's tour of that country in 1943, is widely regarded with suspicion. As is the Uraguayan Inter-Cities Competition, 1964 (Runners-up). And few people at the club have very clear memories of the club's alleged 4–0 victory in the Final of the All-Lapland Under-26 Invitation Trophy, 1966. Although Paddy O'Guinness says he has clear recollections of a relationship with an Eskimo bird around that time; "It got so hot, the Igeeolera, or whatever they call it, started to melt, begorrha!" he told me.

Some of the honours are clearly open to doubt; "The Floodlit Junior Cup 1964—Almost Winners" and "FA Junior Cup, 1956, Robbed".

Letters To The Editor

The programme, in general, is full of useless statistics like how many games Sid Trowbridge played for the club before being transferred to Wittingham Town Wanderers at the start of the 1927 season. It is full of letters from silly 13-year-old boys who want to know how many goals Paddy O'Guinness has scored with his left foot, on away grounds, while wearing his false teeth? Then there are letters from creepy, intelligent 14-year-olds, sharp-eyed sleuths who have spotted a mistake in last week's programme; Ham United won their game against Ackers Town 3–1, in 1906, and not 2–1 as stated. Letters are also received from boring old men of 110, who claim to have known famous historical Ham United players in their youth. Such letters invariably trail off into meaningless ramblings about eating pie and chips in the "Old Days" for a penny, and how Jackie Muddlethorpe was the greatest centre half that ever lived, and would have given these youngsters today a right run-around if he had survived the trenches.

The Trainer's Jobs

The job of the club trainer is to sit in the dugout on the touch-line at every game, and shout abuse at the players throughout the game. Some not so wealthy clubs employ part-time trainers to come in on Saturday to do this. Among the trainer's secondary duties are things like actually training the team—this involves giving Mugsy life size pictures of next week's opponents so he recognises by Saturday who to kick.

Souvenir Shop

The club souvenir shop sells everything that the local fan could ask for—locks of Vincent's hair, gristle off Mugsy's shin, and machetes in the team's colours. Also, car stickers such as "I'm a

Ham United fan. Stop me and let's have a punch up". And this week's special offer at the souvenir shop; broken bottles, in crates, available to anyone who can prove he is a member of the Skull End by bringing in a limb of last week's opponents.

Groundsman

The club groundsman is a football fan who never made it as a road painter—he kept painting centre circles at T junctions, and penalty spots in the middle of the road. Then he was finally spotted. The Chairman, passing by in his Rolls Royce, driven by his personal assistant and chauffeuse, Miss Suzy Goodtime, saw Sid painting a delightful centre circle on a dual carriageway, and decided that the club must have this man. The Chairman is proud of his talent spotting.

Old Fred Is Still At The Club

The close season is when most clubs like to do their ground improvements such as extend the Directors' Car Parks, re-stock the Chairman's Bar, and feed the rats in the visiting team's dressing room. Minor considerations such as re-turfing the pitch, and providing more amenities on the terraces for the supporters are left to the whims of Old Fred, the club's resident caretaker for the past 40 years. Old Fred is one of the veterans from the old days, whom successive Managers have been unable to chase out of the woodwork. He is in charge of the safety and maintenance of the ground, except the important bits like the Directors' Bar, which is the concern of Hubertoid, the head commissionaire. And the Chairman's Bar, which is the sole concern of the Chairman's personal, private secretary, Miss Suzy Goodtime.

Fred's Checks For Safety

Old Fred takes hours to paint the centre spot on the pitch, from which the ball is kicked off at the start of every match. He often has to be dragged away from his labour of love just as the first game of the season is about to kick off.

Old Fred is proud of the vigilance he displays in overseeing the condition of the ground. He reckons to make a complete circuit of the ground, checking the safety of the crush barriers, and the strength of the structure, nearly once a season. Checking the safety of the crush barriers means Fred leaning his hardy eight-stone frame against each barrier in turn, and marking it off on his check sheet as "sound", if it has not collapsed after five seconds. He gives the girders a tug as he passes them, to assess them too. For cleanliness, he takes a feather duster to the terraces at the start of the season, and then again at the end. Also in the cause of spectator comfort, Fred takes a hose to the terraces after every home game, to wipe off the blood, but as he says "There's so much of it, there's not much you can do, is there? Reminds me of the trenches on the Somme. When I was in the first war . . ."

We will leave Old Fred there for a minute, and come back in a couple of paragraphs, by which point he should have finished his reminiscences.

Bottle Mania

Ham United, like all English Football League clubs, like to provide a wide ranging selection of facilities for their spectators. These consist of five (sometimes) flush toilets—"Bring your own paper"—and seven latrines, among 40,000 people. For liquid refreshments, there are four bars, each capable of holding up to $26\frac{1}{2}$ people, where you pay 30p for the privilege of drinking light ale from plastic mugs in Ham United colours. The club also operates a nice little racket with bottles, which are illegal on English Football Grounds, since they are potential weapons against the Chairman's Rolls. But most people would rather drink out of bottles than the plastic mugs the club is so thoughtful in providing, and patrons may obtain light ale, as drunk by Robby, at slightly more than 30p. Any person found taking a bottle out of the bar is fined £5 on the spot for carrying an offensive weapon.

Our Own Crest

The neon sign above the entrance is another of the Chairman's kind gifts to the club, something which nobody is ever allowed to forget. The "Ham United" sign continues into "Also wear a Knowlesworth truss". The Chairman had to be restrained from putting the Knowlesworth crest on the team shirts, by the Committee of Pompous People in Charge of Football, who thought it would bring the game into disrepute. Which is a phrase they have for anything being done by anyone in the game that they do not like. The Chairman had to settle instead for life size portraits of the team scattered around the pitch, wearing Knowlesworth trusses. The Knowlesworth crest is, however, stamped on all club soap, jock straps and boot laces.

The most recent addition to the ground facilities, in which Ham United take so much pride, is the Chairman's underground Rolls Royce car park, complete with massage parlour, operated for the Chairman's personal convenience by Miss Suzy Goodtime, his personal private masseuse and business associate.

The underground excavations were originally intended for a gym for the players so that they could train in comfort on rainy days. But as the Chairman so rightfully pointed out, "Players have been training in the wind and snow and all the rest of it for years, and we don't want to start pampering them now, do we?"

The Chairman's Pep Talk

The Chairman keeps in touch with the chaps by talking to the players at least twice a season. That is, on the opening day of the season, when the entire first team squad, minus Mugsy, who disgraced himself on one of these occasions a few years ago, troop into the Chairman's office for sherry and a pep talk. Here, sipping the Chairman's personal vintage sherry, expertly served by Miss Suzy Goodtime, personal assistant and wine taster to the Chairman, they listen spellbound to the Chairman's rambling discourse on the need for team spirit, and what it was like in the trenches, and how they must all bear in mind that they are responsible not only for the Good Name of Ham United Football Club, but also for that of Knowlesworth trusses and pogo sticks. By the time the Chairman falls into a druken stupor, and, for the third time, starts rambling about how difficult it is to keep servants these days, the players feel able to slip out of the office without trouble, stopping briefly to give a pinch on the bum of Miss Suzy Goodtime, personal private assistant extraordinary, and all-purpose groupie to anyone earning over £10,000 a year.

Since he is a particular enlightened Chairman, Knowlesworth-Blair also speaks to the players in the event of the team winning something. Usually, his words on these occasions consist of something like, "Well, I suppose you buggers now think you are entitled to something like a Win Bonus, hey? Well, just because everyone else gives these things, that is not to say that we have to, you know".

Under great pressure, and the threat of a players' strike, the Chairman usually relents and pays out a bonus of Knowlesworth trusses and pogo sticks.

Where They Play

No football ground is sited at random. Great thought goes into the siting of every Football League ground; more thought, it might be said, than goes through the average footballer's head in a lifetime. Blood Park, the homely ground of Ham United Football Club, is no exception. It is situated within kicking distance of the local mortuary, and the Rolls Royce servicing workshop for the Chairman's car. The club's Chairman, on choosing a site for the ground, always sees to it that it is situated away from those three temptations of the flesh that footballers are more prone to than us mere mortals; namely betting shops, public houses, and naked ladies of ill repute.

Sometimes, however, the decision on the siting of a ground is left to the Manager. This is why so many players like to become Managers—so that they can build training grounds in the vicinity of such sorely-needed facilities, while they can still profitably remember what they are for.

The Directors' Selfless Duty

Most Directors would hate it to be thought that they exert pressure in any way on the Manager in the rightful execution of his duty. They merely require him to appear before them after every defeat, and after prostrating himself at their feet for several minutes, to stand with match ball and chain around his ankle, until he is adjudged to have given a satisfactory explanation for all recent upsets and embarrassments. This is because Directors are a breed of people who have a passionate interest and involvement in The Game and the continued satisfaction of the club's followers; not at all because they are very rich people who seek a cheap form of prestige to exhibit in front of their drinking colleagues at the Lots of Money Club, Whitehall, London. It is also because of their selfless devotion to Soccer that most Directors like to have their names printed in big bold type at the front of the club's match-day programme, to have new stands named after themselves, and constantly to have their photographs taken holding the club's latest honour, or if the club has not won an honour lately, holding the decapitated head of the unfortunate Manager.

Director Smith-Jones runs the clubs' Saving Scheme for supporters. Supporters put their life savings into the club, which saves them the bother of looking after it, or of ever hoping to see it again.

No club is complete without its Backroom Boys, or if the players' sexual inclinations are of a more orthodox nature, Backroom Girls.

Safety Gear From The Souvenir Shop

The club's souvenir shop sells bullet-proof long johns, poisoned darts, and tape recorded sound effects of a big mob of mates, useful when confronted with several hundred Skinheads at an away ground with no help in sight. One may indeed purchase one's own personal bodyguard of Skinheads, freshly cropped and ready for action. But these are obtainable only from Renta-thug, London.

Normal club souvenir shops do not like to be too concerned with such nasty folk, particularly if there is no money to be made from them. However, the souvenir shop does sell spokes to mount on the wheels of your motor bike, that will automatically tear the tyres of motor cars to shreds, at the flick of a button.

Footballers normally have Monday off, to recover from the previous Saturday's game. This is opposed to the other days of the week, when they have it off. Then they return to training on Tuesday when they have to relearn football completely, because the two-day break has been too much for most of them, and has siphoned away what knowledge they ever had of The Game.

Fans Of The Past

Football Clubs like to have a tradition. Because if you can lay claim to a string of famous old players from years gone by, you get all the old men coming along to watch the present side, in order to run them down continuously in comparison with their boyhood heroes. Which the club does not mind at all, so long as the old moaners are paying to come along and have their moan. To accommodate this sort of supporter, clubs have what are called 'Croakers Enclosures', where every miserable, muttering old windbag, who hates the sight of the modern game, can sit with his fellow sufferers and moan and croak continuously during the whole game. Sometimes clubs have to give nearly half of a whole stand to their 'Croakers Enclosure'.

This is a bit of a problem to modern clubs, who in some cases have to stoop to inventing traditions, including their own Hall of Fame to attract this kind of supporter.

A glorious club tradition is useful in other ways too; it is an added attraction to visiting American tourists. "My goodness, Hubert!" one was heard to exclaim to her spouse while they were walking round on one of the club's tours for foreign (rich) tourists. "The club's history goes all the way back to 1927, it says here. Do you think Henry Tudor ever came down to watch them?"

An alleged glorious tradition also gives the Manager another stick with which to beat his hapless players. "You wouldn't have stood knee high to the team of 1907" is a common cry in clubs whose earliest history probably dates back to 1910. Present players are unflatteringly compared with mythical players of the past, whose exploits are endlessly recited by an admiring Manager, obviously sorely jealous that he never got his paws on such a talented outfit.

An American Takeover Bid

However, such illustrious traditions are also responsible for one of the major occupational hazards of football—takeover bids from rich Americans who want to buy up the entire club, break it up into little pieces, and ship every stud over to America to rebuild it there on their private estate the size of Wales. This season, Ham United have spent much time trying to fob off the friendly approaches of Jed. J. Jerkhoff III from Phoenix, Arizona, who wants to ship Ham United over to his "small plot of land back home", as he is given to calling his Arizona ranch twice the size of Scotland.

Jerkhoff's interest in football is no passing fad; his Great, Great, Great, Great, Great Grandfather was a left half who travelled over to America with the Pilgrim Fathers on *The Mayflower*. (There was a great refereeing purge at the time, and many a God-fearing wing half was forced to cross the Atlantic if he wanted to live his life the way he chose.) Jed buys up a different English Football Club every time he visits the "old country".

A Present For Martha

It is to re-assert his English heritage that Jed wants to cut Ham United up into little pieces, ship it across water, and assemble it in his Arizona desert, next to his English cathedral, English pub and English stately home. (It also keeps his wife happy, when he returns every year from his protracted business tours of Europe, if he brings her a little something just to prove he has not been consorting with naked ladies of ill repute while away.) Martha just loved her English cathedral last time, although it remains to be seen what she will think of the collection of crooks, groupies, sadists, till-dippers and hooligans that make up Ham United.

Scattered throughout the club's infrastructure are a number of aged, wizened veterans, who have long since hung up their boots, but whom successive Managers have been unable to chase out of the woodwork. Prominent among these are Old Bert, Charlie Chidthorp, and Old Harry Sidebuckle. Old Bert is a particular problem, because he keeps cropping up at the end of the first team as they run out on to the pitch at home games.

The reason that no Manager has ever dared run them out of the club is because they have been there for so long they now know enough of the murky dealings at the club to feed the press with scandals for several seasons. They would prove more of an embarrassment to the club by talking to the press, than they are hanging around the ground all day like grumbling ghosts. So instead, they have been given genteel jobs like feather dustering the terraces at the commencement of the season, manning the Players' and Directors' Bars on match-days, and parking the Chairman's Rolls Royce. The club pays them a reasonable weekly stipend to supplement their pensions, and keep them quiet.

However, the veterans rarely fulfil their duties, but spend the week shuffling around the stadium and training ground, muttering about "Long-haired Little Yobbos who would never have made the 1933 side", and "The Good Old Days".

Then come Saturday, they take their place with their compatriots in the 'Croakers Enclosure', for a full 90 minutes whining and groaning about the modern game. The average Croaker is an old man of 97, who usually had some dim, distant relationship with a Ham United hero of 50 years ago. He constantly compares his hero to the "Long-haired Selfish Little Brats who are playing the game now".

Ever mindful of the economic difficulties of the game, most clubs are ever mindful to be economic in their work. This means that while the Chairman and Directors travel first class to away matches, the teams are booked on to overnight coach journeys, or may even have to thumb their way to matches on long distance lorries. As Chairman Knowlesworth-Blair told me at the start of the season, "Got to watch the pennies, you know. Lots of people in the game, always very ready to be irresponsible with other people's money. That's why I make sure that all the money in the club is mine. If it isn't my money when it comes into the club, it certainly is by the time it leaves the club. Gives one a sense of responsibility in the face of so much power, you know !"

Financial Worries

Club finances are a matter of great privacy in football. Football clubs do not for the most part believe in silly nonsense like yearly statements, or the opening of accounts to public scrutiny. This is a reflection of the great esteem that football authorities hold in financial circles. It is part of their mystique, and an important part of their overall code of honour.

As Director Smith-Jones told me, pausing to withdraw his hand from the till, "Football clubs are run on similar lines to that other great people's institution, The City. A man's word is his bond, you know," he told me. "If we say that our finances are all right, and we say we have enough money to buy some high-priced chappie from somewhere or other, then we expect the other club to take our word for it. Can't have snotty-nosed accountants, or some reporter type poking his nose into our affairs; it would destroy the faith that clubs have built up tirelessly over centuries."

Or, as Chairman Knowlesworth-Blair put it when I enquired more deeply into the club's financial dealings : "Bugger off ! It's none of your bloody business", before falling comatose on the floor, and being wheeled into his private resting room at the club, by Miss Suzy Goodtime, his personal private assistant and accountant. Directors are very touchy about the subject of their own private contributions to the club's income, which is why they merely mention it by having new stands named after themselves.

It's A Queer World

The member of the backroom staff who has to have the closest liaison with the players is the club physiotherapist. It is his job, in addition to keeping the players' bodies tuned up from day to day, to nurse players back to fitness after injuries from assorted nasties on the pitch. He has to spend hours at a time massaging tired muscles back, and manipulating weary limbs into shape. Word of this seems to have got around to some very odd quarters indeed; whenever a club advertises a vacancy for a physiotherapist, hordes of applications on pink scented notepaper are received from people with names like Julian, Crispin and Audrey.

Poofs trying to break into football are nothing new; every now and again, clubs consider changing their playing-strip colours. It helps when a club is striving for a new image, and it can fool the home spectators into believing that they are watching a completely different team from last season's load of old rubbish. But whenever it becomes known that a club is striving for a new image, hordes of letters pour in, with elaborate designs for Masher's jock strap, a pink suede shirt with matching handbag for Vincent, with numbers in chrome silver, gold lamé knee-length shorts, outlined in sequins.

At times like these, fashion whizz kids send in suggestions that if Masher would only dye his hair purple, and Robby wear eye make-up to match the colour of his bootlaces, then for sure Ham United's recent run of away defeats would come to an end. Art students send in designs for two-tone shorts, boots with platform heels, and see-through shirts. The suggestions are invariably refused, with a curt rejection slip.

However, football has one legendary story of a poof who made it as far as Trainer. He sat on the trainer's bench, throughout the match, expectantly fingering his trainer's bag, a gold lamé hand-bag, to match his track suit, waiting anxiously for the first team member to hit the deck and require his tender attentions.

CHAPTER FOUR

The Game

The chapter they did not want to publish! Read it, and you will see why! They said this chapter had nothing to do with a book about football! They said that in the age of Bunny Girls, footballers' agents, superstars, skinheads, sociologists, psychiatrists, social workers, ghost writers, and night clubs, there is no place in football for playing football. What's 90 minutes on a Saturday afternoon, to a great game like football? So I apologised, and after writing this chapter, said that although such a description of a game of football had nothing to do with The Game as it is understood in modern times, would they please publish it as a personal favour towards me and my aged grandmother in Scunthorpe, and her pet budgie, whom I have to support?

Overture: Entry Of The Skinheads

The build-up to a football match may be viewed as a vast human interaction, a ritual with roots going back to the primeval dawn of history. At approximately 2 o'clock on every Saturday afternoon, thousands of uniformly dressed young men emerge from the station, carrying symbols of their basic and deep-seated dissatisfaction with the underlying precepts and principles of modern society, namely axe handles and sharpened steel combs. Passers-by huddle behind cars and in doorways, programme sellers take a sudden deep interest in the contents of their wares, while these primeval warriors pass by on their way to their religious festival, the highest expression of their innermost and intrinsic feelings.

When things have died down, and the Skinheads have passed by, thousands of Sociologists and Psychiatrists emerge from the station to take their reserved places in the stand, and observe from there the latter stages of the rituals that they are so careful to avoid in the open streets.

Before beginning this commentary on a typical Ham United

home game, one must note in passing, how bloody stupid the whole thing is. Here are 22 able-bodied men kicking a ball about, when they would be better off down the pit, egged on by 30,000 barely-suppressed savages, who would be better off staying at home and beating their wives. (The barely-suppressed savages include 4,000 Bovver Boys who would be better off smashing windows and hanging around street corners.) Football matches are an irrelevancy in other ways too; for one thing, they distract the police from their normal duties. It is common knowledge that the crime rate soars at Ham United's home games while the police are busy sorting out the Bovver Boys. Which is why so many professional criminals urge their offspring to take a healthy interest in soccer and thus help daddy get on with his work undisturbed.

The Pre-Match Build-up

By 2 o'clock on Saturday afternoon, all the players have arrived, having dispatched their companions to the wives' enclosure or the groupies' enclosure, whatever the case may be, and then the entire first team are locked into the dressing room.

At a quarter past two, Jock McNivers works his way down from the Directors' Bar, where he has been anxiously haggling over details in his forthcoming four-year contract, to supervise the build-up to kick-off.

The players get changed, chatting lustily to each other about the previous week's events, and next week's wife-swopping rota. All that is, except Davy, still very shy, who goes off to change in the Gents.

All the players are engaged in the personal rituals that help them to take their minds off the task ahead; Barclay is in one corner, practising his overhead cucumber flick; Robby Score is combing his golden locks in front of the mirror, while Jock is filling up the emergency flasks of whisky that he distributes around the touchline for quick nips during the game. Paddy is going around, anxiously hustling spare stand tickets off the other players, for all the folks from the pub whom he invited over to the game while he was drunk the other night. Robby is now exercising by kicking a ball against the wall, while Mugsy is exercising by kicking the wall repeatedly with his stockinged feet.

At half past two, the changing room falls quiet; it is time for the Manager's pre-match team-talk. This is an important moment in football; it marks the culmination of the week's preparation for the match. If the players do not know which opponent they have to kick by now, this is their last chance to find out. After this they are on their own. There will be nothing more that Jock can do.

The Match Tactics

After screaming a few generalities at them in his broadest Scots tongue, to remind them who is boss, McNivers gives a final run down on this afternoon's opponents, their anticipated moves, known weaknesses, and normal tactics, and how he wants Ham United to respond. Then he goes to each Ham United player in turn, telling him what he wants him to concentrate on that afternoon. Sid is told to pay particular attention to the opposing centre forward's ribs, while Mugsy is detailed to take care of his ankles.

He warns Vincent that the opposing centre half is "even thicker than . . ."; he almost says "Mugsy", but stops himself just in time. He hastily re-phrases his sentence to "most centre halves". So he tells Vincent that if he stands around in the penalty area for long enough, he will be sure to get at least three or four penalties.

Jock reminds Sid that the winger he is marking has a deceptive body swerve, so to watch him very carefully. Sid nods. He is not worried; he has been developing a deceptive clog, in preparation, all week. And finally, Jock tells Davy not to be upset about the nasty things that opponents say to him. They don't really mean them. Robby Score is told that the inside right whom he is marking makes a speciality of jumping for high crosses; a quick one in the knackers should be a sufficient deterrent there.

Brains is warned that it is rumoured that this team occasionally fields an intelligent midfield ball player, like himself, thought to have nearly three O levels. This afternoon may lead to a stern contest of intellects in this department, usually Brains' unquestioned prerogative.

After the detailed run-down, McNivers screams his usual ten minutes' worth of incomprehensible dire warnings, encouragement, threats, insults, praise and damnation, finishing with an audible line in neo-English! "If yu no win, yu need no come bac!"

With a final snarl, McNivers turns to leave his players, by now quaking in their jock-straps, pausing only to throw Robby the $\frac{1}{2}$p piece that the captain uses in the toss up at the beginning of the match. "And I wanna it back after the game, yu hear?" He storms off to watch the match from the comfort of the Directors' box.

Where Does The Manager Sit?

Some Managers like to sit in the dugout on the touchline, and join the trainer in screaming abuse at the players for a further 90 minutes. But Managers who still feel somewhat insecure in their appointment, tend to like to sit in the Directors' Box for matches. In this way they can talk their way out of ghastly errors, such as own goals, and punch-ups which the team lose.

Also, of course, it is very easy to impress Directors, whatever the state of play, with your deep knowledge of football. Directors, one should remember, know basically nothing about The Game. You can tell them that a 0–0 draw is merely an early stage in the master plan you have devised to dominate the away game later in the season. And you can say that a 5–0 defeat is a tactical move designed to induce over-confidence in next week's opponents.

Also, a seat in the Directors' Box gives you a bird's eye view of the

Skull End, and of the fights therein, and by observing the more troublesome members of that part of the ground, you can often spot the centre halves of the future, as Policemen go sprawling from the flourish of bovver boots.

Out On To The Field

At ten minutes to three the team leaves the dressing room, to start the long walk to the tunnel entrance to the pitch. On the way, they pass the referee's dressing-room, when everyone is careful to knock on the door, peer round grinning broadly, and drop a remark like "Good day!", "Do have a nice game!", "Oh, dear! Look, I've dropped a ten-pound note on the floor at your feet!" "Lots of free birds at the celebrations after we have won this game; you should come along!" Even Mugsy manages to muster a grin as he manoeuvres his 22 stone frame around the door for a few brief social pleasantries.

At this stage in the proceedings, the two teams sometimes meet in the tunnel. Wise managers try to avoid this, because it can mean the punch-ups starting even before the players have got out on to the pitch. And it can look rather bad if four of your players come out limping on one leg, with a bleeding nose and two black eyes.

But this time things have gone well, and Ham United can tell from the chorus of boos and jeers, and the tinkle of pennies tearing into flesh, that Muggingthorpe have reached the pitch ahead of them. Pausing a few seconds for the crescendo to die down, Robby leads his men out into the hot afternoon sun, and the welcoming cheers of the 30,000 odd mugs, bovver boys, croakers, spivs, poofs and silly little boys who have turned up for yet another boring home game.

What follows now, is called the pre-match kick about. This is not, as the name might suggest, a warm-up for the personal feuds, vendettas and punch-ups that will flow throughout the match itself. It is instead, ten minutes or so when the teams kick practice balls around among themselves, to remind the players what they are out here for in the first place.

They do this in their respective halves of the pitch. However, when balls stray over into the opponents' half of the pitch, mishaps sometimes do occur, because opponents see the whites of each other's eyes, and get the afternoon's proceedings off to a premature start.

At about two minutes to three, the referee and his two linesmen run out on to the pitch, to a ripple of applause from the posh spectators and the players temporarily revert to playing football.

The Toss

The referee calls the two captains to the middle of the pitch, and asks them to shake hands, toss a coin to decide who will have choice of kick-off or playing direction. Kick-off does not mean allowing

someone to have the first foul with impunity, but who will be allowed to kick the ball off from the centre circle. Most captains who win the toss choose which way they will play in the first half, and take care to choose the end which means that their opponents will be facing the sinking sun in the latter half of the game. And preferably with the home end to their backs. A few grunts are then exchanged, and the teams take up their positions.

Linesmen in Position

Linesmen tend to be failed semaphore signalmen or frustrated referees. Their job is to run up and down the touchline, waving their flag in the air whenever they see that the ball has gone over the line, or spot a nasty on a player, that the referee has not seen. They are also meant to help the referee with the interpretation of the Offside Law, by keeping a watchful eye on the foremost attackers of both sides. But as no one in football really understands the Offside Law, this duty tends to get neglected. The three officials dress in black, but linesmen tend to be black and blue on their reverse side, where they catch it from flying missiles, orange peel and beer cans from the crowd.

Another of the referee's jobs is to see the photographers off the pitch at the start of the game, to their allotted posts behind the goal nets.

Psychological Photographic Warfare

There is a bit of psychological warfare involved here. Photographers obviously like to get behind the goal where they expect most goals to be scored. Clubs often use persuaders like a fully stocked Press Bar, or £10 notes, to influence the photographers' choice of ends. When Ham United have a particularly hard home game, and it is obvious that all the photographers will be gathering behind the home goal, Chairman Knowlesworth-Blair ropes in several Knowlesworth employees for a day's 'voluntary overtime', equips them with cameras, and dispatches them to stand behind the opposition goal for the afternoon. This usually just about balances the hordes of press photographers who are gleefully congregating behind Fingers in the Ham United goal.

This particular League match is not a problem, however. There is only Old Joe from the local paper, who, for the price of a shandy, can always be expected to turn his camera only on the more favourable action of Ham United. As usual, there is Old Arthur, the club programme hack who dutifully takes up his position behind the Muggingthorpe goal; a group of society photographers who have come to take aesthetic pictures of Vincent's body-swerve; and a young university chappie who has been given a pass to pursue his theory, by photographs, that Masher gives 22.7 hefty upfield clearances with his left boots for every 17.9 incisive forward balls played by Brains.

Kick Off

The toss-up ceremony finished, the teams take up their positions, Robby stopping off on the way back to his position in the heart of the defence to wind up Mugsy. The referee's whistle is now awaited to signal the start of the proceedings. Ham United kick off in their normal adventurous fashion, with Vincent taking the kick, passing it to Brains, who pushes it out to Barclay, who passes it back to Brains, who passes it back to Robby who passes is back to Fingers. Up in the Directors' Box, tough, new breed of manager, hard-talking, no-nonsense, Jock McNivers smiles; 30 seconds gone and so far they have not conceded a goal.

Fingers throws the ball out to Sid Scythe, who boots it upfield to Vincent, who is booted to the ground by his opponent. As this is only the first diabolical nasty of the game, and we are still in the first ten minutes, the referee takes no notice, and waves play on. Most referees like to give teams a ten minute settling down period at the start of a match. Most teams gratefully take this opportunity, and settle down to kick the hell out of the opposition for ten minutes with perfect impunity. The first player to be caught and booked for it is regarded as a big sissy.

By now the ball is back with Brains, who spots that Barclay is the only United forward not involved in a niggling match with his opponent. Brains quickly directs a knee high cross to the talented winger who, pausing only to flick the ball up on to his thigh, and sail past the opposing right back who is lying on the floor flailing away with his studs in a vain late tackle, advances towards the goal. Barclay nimbly rounds the goalkeeper and flicks the ball into the net for a goal.

Jubilation Short Lived

He turns away, arms raised, and joins his mates in the two and a half minutes of unleashed sensual joy that traditionally follows a goal. However, the referee with much arm-shaking and whistle blowing has disallowed the goal for Offside. It was not Offside of course, because, as you will remember, nobody in football understands the Offside Law. But the referee decides that he has been giving the balance of the fouls against Muggingthorpe, another common characteristic of the wise referee. So it would be grossly unfair to give a goal against them, at this stage, as well. The referee is the one person who is required to appear to know what the Offside Law means. He has already let Mugsy get away with several Super Nasties off the ball.

An Incensed Crowd Reacts

There now follows one of the traditional rituals of football, with the crowd roaring with anger, at the disallowed goal, and the Skull End singing a little ditty which reflects on the authenticity of the referee's father. The Ham United players crowd around the referee using some of their well practised phrases from the previous week's training—"Oh ref!!" "Wot was wrong with that then?" "It was never offside!"

After this has gone on for five minutes, Robby, as captain, manfully intervenes, and clears the players away from the referee, pausing to whisper aside to the little man in black : "One more like that, and you've had your bottle of Scotch, you short-sighted little git!"

Skulduggery On The Pitch

Meanwhile, the Muggingthorpe trainer has taken advantage of the diversion to sprint on to the pitch and dash around the defence sharpening up his players' studs with a blunt file, and adjusting the goalkeeper's knuckledusters. The game resumes with the Muggingthorpe goalkeeper taking a goal kick; because while no one knows what the Offside Law is, everybody knows that the solution for transgressing it, is to give the goalkeeper a free kick.

The game continues for another 20 minutes, before the next noteworthy incident. Mugsy goes to kick his opponent, misses, and kicks

the ball instead, which catches the Muggingthorpe centre forward
in the knackers, and not surprisingly sends him sprawling in the
mud. (One should mention here, that it is traditional when a clogger
lays low a ball player, he turns to the crowd for the traditional
thumbs-up or down, to decide whether or not he should carry on
and break his leg. If a clear cut decision does not emerge, the
decision is referred to an independent panel of retired cloggers and
TV commentators.)

Mugsy Booked For Kicking The Ball

Mugsy goes over to help the man to his feet, gently pulling him
up by his ears, accidentally trampling on his ankles, exciting further
screams of agony from the unfortunate man. In his panic the referee
blows up, and books *both* men.

All the players are very incensed by this. These are very elemen-
tary fouls, and no self-respecting professional footballer would get
caught doing such minor nasties as this. Mugsy, in particular, is
most offended; "That's nuthin' " he grunts. "I can do 'em much
better'n that," he is muttering as Robby wisely pulls him away from
the vicinity of the ref. Brains meanwhile has come over to give
Mugsy's name to the referee for booking, another of the invaluable
ways Brains helps out his intellectual inferiors in the defence.

Half Time

Soon it is half time, and the teams troop off the pitch to delirious
applause from the crowd, and some particularly ecstatic applause
emanating from the Directors' Box in a broad Scots' accent.
McNivers is overjoyed; they have not given away a goal; none of
them has been sent off yet; they have chopped their opponents
mercilessly, and so far have had only one booking. Already, Jock
sees glimmers of the League Championship ahead.

The teams stagger back to their respective dressing rooms,
exchanging a few cursory blows on their way down the tunnel. The
Ham United players collapse on to their benches, and gnaw
oranges while waiting anxiously for the Manager's verdict on the
first half. All except Jock Maul, who sneaks into the showers for a
quick nip of the old malt whisky, and Davy who drinks from the
thermos flask of lemonade that his mother has so thoughtfully
provided for him. Then the gnawing of oranges and sipping of drink
stops, and silence reigns, while the team wait timidly for their
Manager's appraisal of their performance so far, to see whether
they should be in a jubilant or downhearted mood.

After a few tense minutes McNivers storms in, gabbling incom-
prehensively. But the players can tell from his tone that he is well
pleased. There now follows the half-time team talk, where the
Manager gives the players a fresh set of instructions, completely
contradicting what he said to them 45 minutes ago.

He ticks off Barclay for scoring the goal and compliments Mugsy on his fouls. This cheers Mugsy up. He had thought that nobody had noticed some of the more devastating crunches he had been doing away from the ball. Brains is told to cut down on the sophistication of some of his forward passes; they are too shrewd for his team mates, let alone for the opposition defence. Jock is told to tighten up on the man he is marking, which means he should start kicking the left shin as well as the right one. Finally, before delving into his shouted exhortations, he says that the Directors were so pleased with the team's first-half performance, that they are considering increasing the No-Lose Bonus. Ham United, like most English teams in the present time, are paid a win bonus, usually about £10. In addition, it is increasingly becoming the habit in the modern game to pay players a further bonus of about £50 if they have not lost. To ensure that the players do not think he is going soft, McNivers screams some customary Manager's abuse at them for two minutes or so, until the bell sounds for the second half.

Second Half

The resumption of the game in the second half can sometimes produce complications; the teams are meant to line up in the opposite sides of the field to which they played in the first half. And defenders of the ilk of Mugsy invariably have to be fetched from the opponents' half of the field, where they have taken up their previous location.

This half it is Muggingthorpe's turn to kick off. Since they have started with the ball, they will obviously try to keep possession of it. This is true of all football teams, but always particularly so of the away team, who are even less interested in scoring goals than the home team. Thus, Muggingthorpe set up elaborate passing moves in their own half of the pitch, well away from any of the Ham United Super Nasties who are likely to do anything diabolical to retrieve the ball.

This goes on for ten minutes before Vincent, Barclay and Davy realise they are not being supplied the ball by their midfield players, while Sid, Jock and Masher realise that they will have to go and get it. Mugsy realises nothing. What follows now is called "Ball Winning". It might more correctly be termed "mayhem" or "murder". (The next paragraph has an X certificate. You have been warned.)

Sid Starts A Punch-Up

The situation calls for one of Sid Scythe's Specials. He launches into a ferocious run from the edge of his own penalty area, arriving, studs first, deep in the Muggingthorpe half, just in time to unleash a devastating tackle on their right half. Unfortunately, the Muggingthorpe right half has not got the ball—the sort of little thing that Sid tends to ignore when launching out on one of his specials. The referee has heard the unfortunate victim's cries of agony and, deciding that everyone else has heard them so he can't ignore them, he strides over in the authoritative manner that referees spend years trying to cultivate, waving his little black book. He calls Sid over to him and calls on the Mugginthorpe trainer to inspect the damage. However, this means that play has to be stopped for a couple of minutes and during this time half a dozen Ham United players congregate around the Muggingthorpe player, stranded on the other side of the field from the referee, and make him an offer he cannot refuse, for the ball. By the time the game is resumed, the player who had the ball has been quietly beaten to a pulp, and Ham United have got possession. The game resumes at a fast and furious pace, while the referee vainly blows his whistle to stop the multiple horrors now being unleashed by both sides. By now, the players are too busy getting stuck in to the best punch-up they have had for days, to take any notice of the referee.

At this point in the game, which is looking particularly goal-less, even by Ham United standards, it is appropriate that we take note of two touching rituals that surround the scoring of goals, two rituals that are in danger of becoming extinct, along with goals themselves, and a fit subject only for anthropologists and other nosy people.

When The Kissing Starts

The first of these touching rituals is the players celebrating the scoring of a goal. The scoring of goals leads to prolonged kissing and hugging sessions which are another cause of the occasional mass intrusion of poofs on to football terraces. When a goal is scored, Vincent, who is usually the culprit in these matters, disappears from view for a full minute, under the heaving, joyful weight of his colleagues. Vincent usually manages to stop the kissing session just in time, when he sees Mugsy laboriously working his way across the centre circle, to join in the celebrations.

When the team really go wild, and score two or more goals, unparalleled scenes of ecstasy sweep across the field; Mugsy and Masher often dance a duet down the touchline, while Fingers swings from his crossbar, and Jock takes advantage of the diversion to sneak into the players' entrance, to snatch a quick swig from the bottle of malt whisky that he keeps concealed underneath the trainer's bench.

And Now The Killing

Another touching ritual of the game, of which we may have seen the very last, is the attack on the referee when the other side scores a goal. It is one of the duties of the referee to note the time of a goal, and enter it, and the score as it changes, into his little black book, always assuming that there is room in his little black book after he has got through the afternoon's bookings. As football became more defensive, and teams were sent out with orders not to score, and not to let the other team score, players got into the habit of eating the referee's little black book, and sometimes the referee as well. When this had gone on too long for the problem to be ignored any longer, the Committee of Pompous People in Charge of Football invented a new pompous sounding rule to cover this particularly nasty eventuality; it was called "ungentlemanly conduct".

Back To The Game

The Skull End is now starting to get warmed up, and screams of agony can be heard mingling with the obscene chants from behind Fingers' goal.

The remainder of the game continues on its boring course long after the last Bovver Boy has sunk his boots into the last handful of spectators who have stayed this long to watch the remnants of the game.

Once the match is finished, the really important things can start. When the last drop of blood has been washed away, players are allowed to leave the changing rooms and give interviews to the pack of howling reporters outside. For this match, the press have selected Masher as the Man-of-the-Match for his decisive tackle that stopped the one move that looked as if it might lead to a goal in the 67th minute.

As Masher emerges from the changing rooms, wiping the last spots of blood from his locks, he is jumped on by a horde of sharp-eyed press boys clutching notebooks, anxious for a quote from the hero of the day. When there has been an undistinguished 0–0 draw in a game, which is fairly standard these days, the press put all the names of the players into a hat, and draw for the Man-of-the-Match. A similar draw is made for the unfortunate mug who has to interview him.

On this occasion, the conversation goes like this:

Dave Swish, *Daily Splurge* reporter: "How do you feel about the result, Masher?"

Masher: "I feel rite chuffed."

Dave Swish: "How do the other lads feel about today's result?"

Masher: "They feel rite chuffed."

Harry Hack, *Daily Bugle*: "Are you at all worried by the fact that this is the 14th consecutive match in which you have failed to score?"

Masher: "Nah, all the boys is rite chuffed that we ain't got beat."

Les Lier, *Daily Stirrer*: "How did the boys feel about Mugsy being booked?"

Masher: "We was all rite sick."

After this weighty exchange has exhausted Masher's intellect, and the reporters' ability to ask shrewd probing questions, Masher moves on to the entrance to the players' car park, where he is ambushed by a horde of television and radio commentators.

The dialogue here is as follows :

Phil Poof, television commentator : "Well, Masher, that was a great game. How do you think the team is playing at the moment?"

Masher : "We are all rite chuffed that we are playing very, very well indeed. Our Manager, Mr. McNivers, is very pleased with us, and we think he is a very, very, good Manager indeed; and we are well chuffed with today's result."

Phil Poof : "Well Masher, that was very interesting. Now we are going to play back the tackle you made in the 67th minute, that almost certainly stopped a certain goal. And a very fine tackle it was, if I may say so. Could you talk us through the replay here?"

Masher : "Yeah, well, like, this coming up on the screen now is the moment when he gets the ball, sort of thing, and starts coming towards me. Know what I mean?"

Phil : "What were you thinking at the time?"

Masher : "I was thinking he's got the ball, and he's coming towards me."

Phil : "That's really sensational, Masher. What happened next?"

Masher : "Well, here, as you see, he's still coming towards me, and I ain't moved yet 'cause my great Manager, Mr. McNivers, has told me never to move when they are coming towards you, 'cause that way they think you ain't got the bottle to make a tackle, like, and so they take it all easy, like. Know what I mean?"

Phil : "What's happening now?"

Masher : "This is the bit where I go to break his leg, but I miss, and get the ball instead. Mr. McNivers was a bit angry about that. He says you should always get them first time, know what I mean? But now, as you see here, I catch him on the knee with me studs when I'm going for the ball, and that sort of makes up for it, dunnit?"

Phil : "How did you feel when you had made that tackle?"

Masher : "I felt rite chuffed."

Phil : "How do you think Ham United will do this season?"

Masher : "I think we are going to have a great season, and our very, very good Manager, Mr. McNivers, says so as well so it must be true. All the boys are well confident about our chances this season."

Then, kicking aside the many small boys who plead for autographs, and groping the beautiful young girls, Masher heads off in the direction of the car park, and towards next week's No-Lose Bonus.

For the statistical minded, those silly people who can only see football matches in terms of useless figures, the statistics of Ham United's home match against Muggingthorpe Town were as follows :

The attendance was 31,000 people—5,678 psychiatrists, 3,253 Bovver Boys, 2,936 society writers, 6,826 plain clothes policemen, 1,798 sociologists, 8,936 silly little boys and about 1,573 croakers. Weapons taken from Bovver Boys entering the gates included 17 tactical nuclar weapons, 48 bazookas, 11 Mills bombs, 14 mothers-in-law and 16 explosive toilet rolls. There were 74 stoppages in the game itself, eight bookings, and two sendings-off.

Weapons thrown at the ref. included 28 sociologists analysing the game, 14 sociologists analysing football crowds and 37 sociologists analysing the effect of crowd disturbances on referees' attitudes and decision-making. And the score? Oh, that was 0–0.

CHAPTER FIVE

How To Become A Professional Footballer

Amazing offer!!! Available only to readers of The Football Handbook To End All Football Handbooks, *and* Bovver Boys *whose parents read it to them every night. A step-by-step guide to becoming a professional footballer; the ideal treat for any youngster, or any oldster who still fancies his chances, come to that. And just to demonstrate our goodwill, here is an extract from this amazing book that will by itself put your son on the road to stardom: "Getting into Football. Step 1: Sleep with the local Club Chairman's wife. If that does not work, sleep with the Chairman".*

See what I mean? Do yourself a service! Do the game a service! And above all, do us a service! Don't miss out on the Soccer Book of the Season. And there is a special Football Groupies' Wallchart to go with the book, a Must for every serious student of the game. Just send £10 and the telephone number of six football groupies, to Rubbishales, Battersea, London. Guaranteed, if you do not become a professional footballer by the age of 17, you get the groupies' phone numbers back. If they've turned out to be right scrubbers, that is.

FOOTBALL clubs sign on a large number of 16-year-old youths when they leave school, and a small number of these become full professionals when they reach 17. However, clubs do not like to miss out on a particularly promising youngster of 15 or 16, and no club is complete without its old hand at forging birth certificates.

Real enthusiasts put their sons down for a football club from an early age, and sometimes even before birth, as with public schools.

Early Training Leads To Success

Real enthusiasts also take care to instil the right attitude in their offspring from the earliest days. Many a successful Soccer star has made it, because in the early days his dad spent hours coaching him in the backyard, refusing to give him his bottle before he had learned to trap the ball. Many a young baby has had to spend half an hour heading and dribbling the ball before he was allowed to go back into his cot for his afternoon's sleep.

And as the youngster grows older, the determined father does not miss a chance to impress upon him his future role in life. Not for the prospective England wing half, the namby-pamby children's toys such as rubber ducks, coloured bricks, and furry Teddy Bears; for him, it must be golliwog strangling, crowbar snapping and endless hours of kicking the hell out of the cat.

Weedy children's foods are soon pushed out, and steak phased in. While walking in the park our infant prodigy is encouraged to growl at other children, particularly those softies who are still being wheeled around in a pram at the age of five months. The thoughtful father makes sure that the lad's wallpaper is appropriate; no cowboys and Indians rubbish, or other sentimental idiocies. Instead, pictures of centre halves downing forwards in horrendous tackles cover the little candidate's walls, and greet him every morning when he wakes up for his six mile run before breakfast.

And when it comes to holiday time, no soppy buckets and spades for our valiant little hero. He spends his time sprinting barefoot with a medicine ball along the shingle beach.

Approach Clubs

However much training the lad does, there comes a time when you, his parent, have to take the first steps in enrolling him in a club. Send him off on one of his thrice-weekly 30 mile runs, and settle down to start writing to clubs, asking that your little boy be given a trial.

Take care to write your first letters to clubs on impressive headed notepaper; this suggests that you are making lots and lots of money, and would be a good person for the club to be involved with.

Open To Suggestions

Always make it quite clear that you are more than happy to bribe them. If you are a used car salesman, for example—and if you are in a business like football, you probably *are* a used car salesman—then you might like to suggest that the Manager has the use of one of your better models during the period in which he has to devote deep thought to the merits of your son for a youth team place.

If you are a turf accountant, which is the posh word for bookie, you make like to offer the Manager unlimited access to your facilities for the period in which he is in deep thought about the welfare of your offspring. If you are an owner of premises frequented by naked ladies of ill repute, you may consider yourself to be well away, and your son to be established in the first team before you can say "corruption".

If, however, the lad's first trial at a club unearths the most unlikely fact that he has some skill, the boot goes on to the other foot, and it is the club's turn to impress you with *their* unrefusable offers. You may now retire from your job and sit back at home while the various unrefusable offers pour in, while every Football League Club in the country does everything possible to make you feel at ease in the difficult period in which you have to make a decision. Many a lucky father has found the torrent of inducements to be so much to his liking, that he has let it flow on until his son is well into middle age.

This is the aspect of the game that invariably brings out the warmth in football people. Parents of especially gifted children find their bank accounts rising to prodigious heights in the period they are considering clubs' various offers. It is in this period, too, that clubs invariably find they have spare tickets for their summer tours, and parents are invited to come along and spend two weeks in Japan with the team, whilst thinking over the whole matter. If this does not sway the balance, other incentives have to be presented by the club; a lifetime supply of Knowlesworth trusses and pogo sticks is a not uncommon incentive to a parent to place his son with Ham United. And it is not at all uncommon for the lucky family to wake up and find a new car in the driveway.

Scouting For Talent

Every club employs a nationwide network of talent scouts, whose job it is to report any likely-looking talent immediately they sight it, and forward all details to the Chairman. The Chairman then selects the 13 most likely-looking lovelies, and has them summoned to Blood Park to re-stock his pool of personal groupies. The club also employs talent scouts whose job it is to discover talented young footballers. If any are discovered, they are told to go away and not to be so silly, and come back when they have learnt to kick the player and not do fancy things with the ball.

A good scout can get fed for life, and have all his needs taken care of, without ever having to do any serious work. All he has to do is merely send in reports now and again of what a great discovery he has made in the local park; then two weeks later, how he has had his discovery filched from right under his nose by a dastardly scout from another club, and would his club please increase his bribery allowance, so that he can get in first next time?

If things get really bad, and the Manager starts screaming for new blood at a time when there is no talent around at all, then Swirdle (Ham United's wizened, elderly, devious chief scout) steals one of the Club's youth team players from a training session and sells him back to the unsuspecting club. Swirdle is reputed to have sold the club its entire youth team forward line on several occasions.

Swirdle spends many hours each week in the homes of parents of likely lads, trying to persuade them to sign their son over exclusively to Ham United. This is usually no problem, because awestruck simple folk listen spellbound for hours to Swirdle's vivid descriptions of what the club has to offer their son, and what life at the top will have to offer him. (Although, as often as not, the club only require the lad in question as an assistant apprentice boot cleaner.)

Swirdle never leaves without giving a few sweeties to the lucky lad in question. The boy is usually unable to accept them person-ally, because he is locked upstairs in his bedroom, screwing a bird and smoking a joint. Nowadays, of course, football does not have the same lure for youngsters that it used to have in the old days. And it is not at all uncommon, when Swirdle is deep in conference with avaricious parents, offering them the best terms that Ham United allegedly have, for the prodigy in question to come trailing into the room, fag in hand and, overhearing what is being discussed, scornfully to turn on his heel, snorting "Ham United! That load of old rubbish!" Or words to that effect.

The Art Of Disguise

An important part of the work of a talent scout is the ability to disguise yourself while at work. This is necessary, because lads who know they are being watched by a scout may suddenly turn on a full-blooded display of maiming and crippling of the opposition to

impress the visiting scout with their professional possibilities. Many a sharp-eyed pansy has been able to get a trial with a club by a smart use of the elbow at the right moment.

However, some scouts overdo the anonymity, and disguise themselves as trees, then give it all away by dashing along the touchline to keep up with play. Swirdle scorns such elaborate measures, largely because he is too thick to think up such schemes. Instead, he prefers to squat on the highest branch of the nearest elm tree, and take a leisurely bird's eye view of the games going on around him in the local parks. The next part of his routine is to dress up in an old plastic mac, wellington boots and downtrodden fisherman's hat, on loan from *The Fishing Handbook To End All Fishing Handbooks*, and then shuffle inconspicuously around the matches.

Every now and again, Swirdle stops his endless wanderings, and sidles up to the Boys' Team Trainer, and says "What's good today, then?" in the hoarse voice much practised by Talent Scouts, so that everyone thinks they have been up all hours of the night, sweating over their labours.

Likely-looking subjects are then asked to say, in not more than six words, why they would like to play for Ham United, and if they fail the routine intelligence test, they are invited along to the ground for the next youth team training session, in the tender hands of Mugsy, or whoever has got too drunk that week.

Moving thus, from match to match, and to and from changing rooms in his decrepit outfit, Swirdle is often taken for another shoddily dressed rover of the marshes, 'The Phantom Flasher'.

Choose Your Club Carefully

Deciding which football club you are going to choose for your son is much like speculating on the Stock Exchange. The club that is at the top of the League at this moment may well be shoring up the rest of the League by the end of the season. While the clubs, who this season are hanging on to survival by their bootlaces, may well be teaching the Europeans a thing or two several seasons hence.

However, the wise father can spot tomorrow's club from today's results, and from a knowledgeable survey of the club's internal structure. All the readers of *The Football Handbook To End All Football Handbooks* are, of course, superbly equipped to spot the club best suited to their son's requirements : an ignorant, egotistical and fabulously wealthy Club Chairman, ignorant, rich, yes-men as Directors, a hard-talking Scots Manager who frightens the hell out of the team, a well balanced, all-round team that rates brains as important as brawn, and includes at least two intelligent players.

However, as these qualities are standard to most football clubs, the wise parent should examine other less obvious aspects of the club's outlook if he wants to be completely sure of his son's well-being.

For example, what sort of scandals do the club's players get involved in? How do they do for Bunny Girls? Is it one of the fun clubs who go to away matches two days early, and get roaring drunk in the hotel in the company of naked ladies of ill repute, or is it one of the killjoy clubs that travel on the day of the match, and whisk their players straight back home again afterwards? Will the club let you, his father and first coach in this great football game we call life, always attend first team games, sitting in the Directors' Box? Will he be allowed to sell his story to the newspapers whenever he feels like it? (And will *he* always remember you, his father, whose valiant and selfless sacrifices enabled him to scale the heights in the first place?)

How He Starts

A prospective footballer, when first arriving at the club at the age of 17, is given a wide-ranging six-minute written examination in English, arithmetic, counting up to four and back again, spelling his own name and learning how to say "I never done it". Anyone scoring more than 2 per cent is sent straight home and told not to be so smart. However, clubs make a practice of retaining one intelligent player, for the purpose of talking to the press and tele-vision, and to be the subject of glowing articles by the club's pet reporter on Brains, the new exciting breed of inside right who proves that the modern footballer is a highly intelligent, sensitive person.

At any time in the first three months of his training, a boy may leave his club, un-fined, if he finds the work distasteful or severely immoral. If he stays on after three months, and then objects to the training methods, he has to sign a form stating that he is a conscientious objector, a lily livered pansy who is not fit to be called a man, or associate with other men, and then buy himself out of the club at any amount the Manager cares to name.

How He Leaves

The only way around this for a young player, is to join a religious sect, and then apply to leave on the basis that the work he is doing violates his religious convictions. But when this started happening on a vast scale, and large numbers of terrified young professionals started saying they could not be a footballer and a Man of God, clubs hastily inserted a 'No-God Clause' in the contracts. After a word of advice from the sort of people who always seem to be around to give words of advice in these situations, this was changed to a 'No-Religion-in-Football' clause. But not in time to stop the Committee of Pompous People in Charge of Football from waking up and saying "Who is this God person, and what right does He think He has to tamper with the structure of the Game as we know it? There are too many outsiders interfering with the game. . . ."

Even so, hardly a season goes by without some moral minded little youngster finding the training more than his conscience can tolerate, and buying himself out at great expense, and then spending the rest of his life in a monastery.

Sometimes footballers seek diplomatic asylum, or sporting asylum in the embassy of a foreign power, and preferably one with a damn good national side and a Manager who approves of naked ladies of ill repute. Otherwise it is not unknown for footballers occasionally to go Absent Without Leave, to slip out from underneath the floodlights, and into the starlit night, never to be seen again.

Such men are looked on as the enemies of society, the lowest of the low, and they have to face a life of social banishment for their failure of nerve. It was for these men that the Foreign Legion, more correctly entitled the Foreign League, was invented. Here, he who deserted his club could start life again, with no questions being asked. Here, only a man's football ability matters, and no questions are asked about his former clubs, tackles he has shirked, own goals he has given away, or the number of times he had had his name taken. Endless games of football are planned in these idyllic surroundings in the middle of the Sahara, under the stars, those great floodlights in the sky. A player here is never forced to say what position he formerly played in; it is a veritable heaven, where referees and abuse from the crowd are unknown. The remainder of the hours while they are not playing football are whiled away with Skinhead hunting and having it off with naked ladies of ill repute under palm trees.

But these pansy conscientious objectors are few and far between, and make up only a small proportion of the footballing population of this country, which was only recently estimated at 67,489,000, with six substitutes.

Check On Your Character

To avoid such tragedies, nasty minded little boys who want to become footballers should always check carefully that they have the characteristics and qualifications to become so, before signing the Indenture Forms for 500 years' service. There are many ways that a prospective footballer can decide if he is suited to the life-style of the hard working Pro. He should study the silly pin-up pictures of footballers in the silly football magazines for silly 13-year-old boys, to see if he can pose in the same way. He should read the very stupid things that players say in the papers, and see if he can say the same things, with feeling. He should watch the way footballers talk through their goals, on television, and see if he can talk through his goals, similarly.

Then the lad concerned should go to a Bunny Club and see if he likes Bunny Girls. And, of course, he should go and find a naked lady of ill repute, and see if he likes her. If our prospective foot-baller measures up to all these arduous tests, he may consider him-self to be made of the stuff that footballers are made of. Whatever that is. (As an added extra, you may learn how to play football, but this is not really important.)

Another essential qualification for the would-be professional footballer is to be able to sit in an air conditioned, de luxe, panoramic view coach, and play cards non-stop on a journey to any away game anywhere in the country. Brains again comes in useful here, because he is called upon to keep a running score of the various accruing debts. He wisely sees to it that the debts are spread evenly amongst the players, so that no ill-will occurs, specifically from Jock Maul, the tight-fisted Scots full back.

Further Education

Football clubs feels they have a deep and meaningful obligation to provide for the continued and extensive education of their youngsters. Every effort is made to broaden the scope of their general knowledge : sweeping the terraces, cleaning the first team's boots, throwing away Jock's empties and polishing the crest on the Chairman's Rolls Royce, are all carefully selected duties that are intended to broaden the average football apprentice's perspective on life.

The early years of any youngster's apprenticeship at a club are always taken up with training. The object of training is to turn sensitive, 17-year-old ball players into fully fledged, nasty minded professionals. Morning training sessions start off with 20 minutes of dribbling practice, followed by heading, tackling, and passing practice. A further 20 minutes are devoted to the tactics that will be used in the next game.

Then all this nonsense is dispensed with, and the rest of the morning is given over to all-in wrestling, kung fu, karate, judo, boxing, unarmed combat, armed combat, rifle practice, as well as general maiming and strangling.

After a break for a brief lunch of steak and steak, training is resumed in the afternoon, with an hour's swearing practice. This is the hardest part of the day's training, and the bit that all footballers dread; they find words an intrusion into an otherwise quite straightforward session. Even swear words that they practise for intimidation purposes. (For really advanced referee intimidation, a whole selection of words are required to be spoken, and most clubs offer extended courses in perming the following words a 100 different ways: "Never!" "Who, me?" "He's faking!" "I slipped." "Me?" The use of words is a new fangled form of training used only by the most adventurous clubs. Most clubs are afraid to try anything new in their training routines, or anything else come to that, since it might bring the Committee of Pompous People in Charge of Football groaning to their feet.

Learning Intimidation

It is a relief to move on from word-training to general intimidation practice, another standard pleasantry practised by all League clubs. Each player faces a full length mirror and spends 30 minutes making the most horrible and grotesque faces that he can summon up. Half an hour's growling and snarling in front of a mirror is guaranteed to bring the biggest pansy up to professional standards in referee intimidation, and opposition smarty-pants forwards. Snarls are developed for every eventuality, and spitting actions are refined to a high point of finesse.

Ham United find that the one problem in using mirrors in training like this, is the club's superstar. If not dealt with carefully, Vincent will spend hours at a time combing his locks and ogling at his own good looks in front of the training mirror. So McNivers makes him dribble endlessly round the other players while they are perfecting their growls, which Vincent likes because it is the one time in training when he is certain of not getting kicked by his team mates.

CHAPTER SIX

How To Become A Superstar

To obtain your free plastic model of Vincent, buy 15 copies of The Football Handbook To End All Football Handbooks, *cut off the top right hand corners, keep these little bits, and send the rest of the book, along with a postal order for £700, to: Uncle Sid, PO Box 301172, Montevideo, Uruguay.*

EVERY CLUB has a Superstar. Even a club with lots of nasties, and no stars, has a superstar. No team would be complete without the face that launched a thousand silk scarves. Superstars are one of those things that have come to be expected of clubs, and who are they to argue with millions of militant 13-year-old girls? They may not even be very good at football, and they are certainly always hated by their team mates who are under strict instructions not to chop the Golden Boy money spinner in training. Most nasties find this instruction very difficult to adhere to, because there is nothing more hateful to a 'chop' merchant than the sight of some namby-pamby silken-haired ball player running rings round the thugs and sadists that make up the rest of the first team squad.

"It ain't natural," grumbled Mugsy, as he barely restrained his steel-capped left boot from Vincent's shining shin, in a practice work-out at the ground earlier this week. Only the Superstar's unique skill, which can result in constant No-Lose bonuses for the rest of the team, saves a Superstar from being massacred by his team mates. Trainers often find it advisable to attach large notices reading "This boy can earn us all an extra £80 a week" to a Superstar, before letting him loose in training with the thugs and sadists.

The Beginning Of A Superstar

Superstars did not happen by accident. Like most things in football, they were invented for a definite purpose. There have always been Superstars, of course, but few of them survive the first day's training at their League clubs, where all the other little boys are anxious to show what they can do with their boots apart from kicking footballs around.

The real wave of Superstars in the game now was invented by Uncle Louis of Consolidated Conmen Ltd. of Lewisham. He thought that the age group that Superstars appeal to most—silly 13-year-old girls—was the one group of fans which the game was missing out. Mums and dads, reasoned Uncle Louis, were already attracted to the game by the odd, homely type of player who has never had his name taken in 45 years of playing the game. Some clubs do have these sort of players, although they are increasingly rare.

Bovver Boys, of course, were attracted by the maniacs and sadists who abound in any healthy football team. They will be a captive audience as long as football remains a blood sport fit only for men. While silly little boys were a guaranteed audience as long as they come along to check that the players look the same as the real players on the bubble gum wrappers of Famous Players and Soccer Stars, that they all prize.

A Snare For Little Girls

But to attract the attentions of hordes of little girls, it became necessary to invent a totally new sort of player. Football has always had the unceasing attentions of big girls, particularly around the Players' Entrance to the Ground, and in the team bath after the match.

To develop this new breed of player to attract silly little girls on to the terraces, consideration was given to re-introducing skill into the game, for the first time since the Roman Empire was sacked by the Huns and Skinheads.

At the idea of an innovation being introduced into the game, the Committee of Pompous People in Charge of Football woke up suddenly and started their customary groans about this threat to the very fabric of the game; "These modern ideas will be the death of the game..." "Dis-service to football..." "Who do they think they are..." But they were reassured that the change was only a temporary and very minor one, so they went back to sleep for the rest of the season.

Off The Drawing Board

However, this decision to bring back skill into the game was taken only with much reluctance and foreboding by the Football Managers. It was only after repeated earnest arguments from the persuasive salesmen of Consolidated Conmen Ltd. of Lewisham and repeated earnest bribes, that Managers began to agree to let the odd ball player emerge untouched from the butchery of practice games, and eventually, into the first team.

Consolidated Conmen were delighted, and before the first Superstar had dribbled his way off the drawing board, they had signed up a whole series of contracts with silk scarf manufacturers, rosette makers, detergent firms, bubble gum manufacturers, and underwear retailers, giving them exclusive exploitation rights in their respective fields.

However, there were complications; if everyone was going to have a Superstar, extraordinary efforts had to be made by each club to keep their particular Goldilocks in the headlines, and thus, for him to continue to be worth his weight in 50p's at the turnstiles. So Superstars were encouraged to be temperamental—not that many of them needed the encouragement.

An essential part of any Superstar's scheme to be temperamental, and indeed, an integral part of his lifestyle, is the great annual runaway. This is really a complete fraud, which the club cannot win. Ham United obviously need Vincent's isolated crop of skill, far more than he needs them. Any advertising agency would pay his weight in tenners for such looks. So the really shrewd Superstar, using the annual runaway as an opportunity to screw a whacking great wage increase out of the club. And he need never worry about abuse from the lads, when he gets back from his wanderings because, being a Superstar, he can afford to have a private gymnasium built into his bathroom.

Vincent Escapes

Vincent's first attempt at the great escape stunt involved his fleeing to a monastery. He found that this was not successful. Religion had been last year's gimmick, with distraught, guilt-ridden centre halves joining all sorts of obscure religious sects, claiming they could not mix their football and religion any more. So instead they moved to monasteries and religious retreats of various sorts, where they started kicking the living daylights out of the monks, instead.

After a three-week delay, in which the club explained Vincent's absence with a series of weedy excuses, to pacify the hordes of weeping girls beating down the door of his landlady's flat every night, the club announced to a startled world that Vincent Spooner had gone absent without leave. At first they had said he had got injured in training. Then they said he had a cold. Then, when he still had not shown up, they admitted he had gone Absent Without Leave, but was expected back shortly. At this news everything changed. Ham United's home gates fell by 20,000, every little girl under the age of 14 stayed off school, sobbing her eyes out, and the discotheques of London emptied overnight, now that people realised they were not going to see Vincent chatting up hostesses of ill repute.

Out Go The Press Boys

Now everything worked as it should. The *Daily Splurge* sent its team of ace investigators, Sid Hack, and Hotpants Harriet, to investigate. Sid sent home pieces in the vein of "Why I had to quit, by Vincent", while Harriet told the world, "I have discovered my real first love." Jumbo jets full of British holidaymakers, made vast detours to fly over the secluded monastery where Vincent Spooner, the poetry writing, crooning, moody Super-star reflects on his future, and also his past.

Vincent's Publicity Manager, Uncle Harry of Consolidated Conmen, thoughtfully set up a toll on the approaching road, so that visiting tourists and natives could for £1.50 spend 10 minutes ogling through the railings at the monastery garden, where at any moment, the slender, boyish figure of Vincent Spooner, the poetry-writing, crooning moody Superstar would be reflecting on his future, and also his past. At least, that is what Harry told them. £2 for 15 minutes.

Then, after a week of saturation coverage in the *Splurge*, Vincent switched his newspaper contract to *The Bugle*, and a rush of stories appeared saying how he was "Sick of all this publicity/Why don't you leave me alone/It's the press who have caused all this to happen/I'm just an ordinary country lad trying to earn a living", etc. etc. And *The Bugle* dispatched *their* ace writer and problem page writer, Aunt Agatha, to write a piece on saying what Vincent really needed was care and love and attention.

After a further week of this, there were no more papers to move on to, except the intellectual papers, so the game was up for another year.

The next stage was The Reconciliation. Telegrams were exchanged with Vincent's Manager, tough-talking, no-nonsense, fire-eating Celt, Jock McNivers. The exchange of telegrams read like this :

"Come back?"	Vincent
"Never!"	Jock "Nailguts" McNivers
"I'll behave"	Vincent
"No extra money"	Jock
"No"	Vincent
"All right"	Jock
"Bit more £££??"	Vincent
"Never!"	Jock
"Won't come back!"	Vincent
"How much?"	Jock
"See Harry"	Vincent

This last remark referred to Vincent's agent, Harry, of Consolidated Conmen Ltd., of Lewisham, London. Harry '20 Per Cent' Sharp stepped forward at this time as an honest broker, to negotiate Vincent's return to football, at an increased rate of pay. Harry now started shuttling back and forth between Vincent's monastery and Jock's tartan-carpeted office, to settle the small print.

A secret meeting was then arranged between Vincent and Jock, Superstar and Manager, on a mid-Atlantic outcrop of rock, somewhere in the Pacific. Here, on a small stretch of land, somewhere off the coast of Argentina, was determined the future of the world's number one ball player, the future success of Ham United's home record and bank balance, and whether Harry would be able to screw enough out of both sides to expand his chain of Pornographic Bookshops.

The meeting was attended by 381 reporters, 176 photographers, 189 sociologists, 96 psychiatrists, 200 TV interviewers and a panel of TV commentators and retired Superstars who judged, with the assistance of action replays, whether the verdict had gone in favour of Vincent or the club. Also present were a referee and two linesmen, and six 13-year-old girl members of Vincent's fan club, who had hi-jacked a jumbo jet to the rock, for the occasion. They stood in the background, attired in their Vincent panties, wailing "Vincent . . . Vin-cent . . . Vin-cent . . ."

Really temperamental Superstars now do not turn up for the meeting, and leave their Manager fuming and tearing up the new contract. However, Vincent knew that in tough-talking, no-nonsense, fire-eating Celt, new breed of Manager, Jock McNivers, he was dealing with an extra specially strong character, so he turned up to the meeting, almost on time.

A tearful reunion was held, where the Superstar said, "I never really meant it, and all I want to do is to spend the rest of my life playing football for Ham United."

And the Manager said, "Yes, son, welcome back. I want you to look on me as your father, and the club as your home, and yourself as part of one big happy family."

The Superstar now gave an interview to the press in which he said he will never, never, never again go out with a girl, smoke a cigarette, drink a drink, go to a night club, run away from the club, frequent betting shops, associate with naked ladies of ill repute, or do anything remotely damaging to the club. He said he would voluntarily go back and live in digs for six months, obeying every word his landlady says, pay penance for all the stupid things he has done, do extra training six times a day.

"I promise never to swear at referees again, only score when I am told to, and in the manner I am told to, and I have the greatest respect for my Manager and I think the press are doing a wonderful job, and what a nuisance girls are, and I really am going to give them up for ever."

The Manager's side of the Reconciliation was for him to come on and say that he had great understanding and sympathy for Vincent's problems, but that to be fair to him, he must be hard on the lad, and so therefore Vincent must go back and live in his former digs for a while, to suffer rule by landlady. Also he was going to confiscate Vincent's transistor radio, and his jigsaw, and his £25,000 sports car.

Vincent was now led away to a round of applause, to the waiting chartered jet, where, once he was aboard, he was tied up, bound and gagged, hand-cuffed, put into a straitjacket and hung, suspended by his knees from the ceiling, until the plane arrived at the club's private training ground, somewhere in the South of England.

Once ensconced here, he was examined by the resident club psychiatrist, who said he was confused. He was then locked in a padded cell with Manager McNivers for six days, while the latter shouted himself hoarse with reprimands and general abuse. A highly chastened Vincent returned to the first team at the next home match, and every silly little girl in the land stopped crying and went back to school—until the next time.

Politics The Next Trend

Superstars are casting around for next year's trendy theme. It is rumoured in those circles where things are rumoured, that next year's In Thing may well be politics, which has most Superstars very worried. Politics is reputed to involve thinking, and that is not good news at all. Still, the hard working gentlemen of Consolidated Conmen, and other similar organisations, are working on it, and slowly coaching their protégés to turn the newspapers back to front, and read the front pages as well.

Vincent, and Superstars like him, have spawned a whole wave of very, very minor Superstars. One may even observe the odd temperamental 11-year-old genius stumping off the pitch at a bad refereeing decision given against him, grabbing his 10-year-old bit of crumpet, and threatening to quit the game for keeps.

How To Get A Penalty

Being a Superstar requires many talents; amongst these, although certainly not the most important, is the ability to play football. But this is no problem when you are faced with a thick, hard-tackling, growling, snarling and entirely stupid opposition defender like Ned Needle of Legcracker Wanderers. Vincent's strategy with Ned is to blow him a kiss at kick-off time, and relax while Ned vainly chases him round the field, for retribution. Or, sometimes he drops a remark like, "Your wife was good the other night—you know, that night you had an evening game." And after that, Ned will be running round for the entire match trying to kick Vincent, and muttering "Get your hair cut, you little Goldilocks pansy", and "I'll strangle you, you little poofda". And Ned's 20-stone frame lurches around the pitch, whilst Vincent weaves his way past his stranded colleagues. Then, when Vincent gets into his opponent's penalty area, he waits for Ned to lumber up breathless to chop him unmercifully to the ground and he's got his team a penalty. Superstars have been using this tactic on Ned Needle for 15 years now, and he still has not realised.

Get Me To The Match On Time

Superstars have to be watched very carefully, because they can forget, while making records, appearing on television chat-shows, modelling underwear and dancing in discotheques at four in the morning, that they are still footballers, and that is what it is all about. Football is full of stories of precocious 18-year-olds who soared into the first team, and after one dazzling display, got so involved in the Good Life that they were never seen again. To prevent this happening, most clubs insist on Superstars having chaperones, rather bulky strong men who tend to be recruited from the strongarm branch of Consolidated Conmen Ltd., to ensure that whatever the little bleeder does in the week, he is deposited in the club's dressing rooms at ten sharp, every Saturday morning, with ball and chain attached to his ankle.

Another important aspect of the Superstar's image is his warm, loving family. Vincent's mum and dad are simple village folk, who shun the limelight, and who have turned Vincent's old bedroom into a museum and are determined to screw every possible penny out of his success.

Harry arranges many press interviews with Vincent's mum, when the lad has done something especially outrageous that is giving him a lot of bad publicity. At these sessions, Vincent's mother sits, as instructed by Harry, quietly supping tea in the small, neat front room of her council house. Carefully primed by Harry, she says things like, "Oh, yes, my Vincent! What a lovely boy! So charming, so sweet and kind, he always was. He was always nice to his dear old mum, you know. I always knew he would do well, of course. And his success has not changed him one little bit; it has never gone to his head, or anything like that. He is still the lad he always was".

Harry always takes care to get such interviews finished quickly, before Vincent's dad gets home, and adds endearing quotes like, "Yes, success has not changed our Vincent at all; he was always a flash little sod. Long haired little git. If I ever catch him round this way, which I very much doubt, I'll break his ducky little neck".

Such threats from ungrateful relations have their compensations, though. Another of the great blessings of being a Superstar is the multiplicity of products that you are asked to put your name to. It is possible to buy Vincent T-shirts, soap, panties, pens, pyjamas, football boots, drinks, whips, jock straps, washing powder and lawnmowers. (While Mugsy is believed to have given his name to a brand of cement somewhere in the Midlands.)

SPECIAL ANNOUNCEMENT: As we suspect that this book has been bought by thousands of silly little 13-year-old girls, who just want to read this chapter about Vincent, and then burst into tears, we are running an extra competition in this chapter. You lucky folks!!! And here it is:

This is your opportunity to win a free Vincent Handbag, in the team colours of your choice. A FREE Handbag, as used by Vincent!!! Just tell us in not less than 10,000 words, how YOU would deal with Vincent if you were his Landlady. Send your suggestions and lots of money to: Harry Sharp, Consolidated Conmen Ltd., The Basement, Bent Street, Soho.

CHAPTER SEVEN

How To Be A Football Fan, Or Survival At A Football Ground

The first thing you ought to consider when thinking about becoming a football fan, is do you really want to become a football fan? If you do, write your reasons, in less than 15 words, in a 4-2-4 formation on a postcard, and send it to: Kick-On-The-Shins, Lancs. Any person becoming a football fan does so at his own risk. You have been warned.

ANTHROPOLOGISTS tell us that football is creating a new breed of man, who hibernates in the summer, and reads the newspapers back to front. While sociologists, on the other hand, tell us that people feel the need to belong to something; political party, army, state, Masons, Buffaloes, VD clinic, football team, or whatever; if they are football fans, they make sure that everybody else is aware of the fact, by wearing steel rimmed bobbly hats, coloured scarves and rosettes, and massacring supporters of other football teams. So much for anthropologists and sociologists; we shall be coming back to them later.

Being a football fan also has its social uses; it gets rid of the week's tensions, and stops a couple of million blokes knocking the hell out of the wife. Instead, it creates every conceivable tension after the match, and creates all the troubles for the next week.

A True Fan

The true fan paints his house the team colours; names his baby after the entire first team squad; puts the team's pictures up at work; and tears his workmates' pictures down; sends the players cards on their birthdays; puts the wife in pawn for games abroad, and hi-jacks a plane to get there; bets his week's wages plus wife's housekeeping money plus wife plus house plus kids plus car, on their Cup chances; says it was a fluke result when they lose and refuses to pay up.

In short, the true supporter not only learns to argue as a supporter of his team, but plans his whole week around the team, not to mention the remainder of his whole life; spends all his time trying to convert other people to his team, and quits his job if his boss supports his own team's deadliest rivals. The true supporter also plans his leisure hours around the team; summer holidays are spent following the team on tour around the world, while Sunday is put to its rightful purpose, resting, in order to develop explanations for the team's failure on Saturday.

The true supporter is not afraid to buy all the little knick-knacks that no true follower would be without; things like a verey pistol, with flares in your team colours, to let your mates know where you are standing. Other essential items are bullet proof vests to repel the missiles from Bovver Boys and lots of £5 notes to placate same if they push you up against a wall and threaten to beat your brains in. (But being a football supporter, you probably have none in the first place, so don't let threats like that worry you.)

Join The Excuses Club

In his efforts to adapt his entire life style, the prospective football supporter has to re-learn his entire vocabulary very early on. This is in order to defend his team against all comers. Your team losing is *unlucky*; your team getting a draw away from home is *earning a point*; the opposition earning a point at your team's ground is *snatching a point*. Your losing a point at home, like that, is *having a point stolen*; your team do not play defensive football—they defend resolutely. Other teams coming and playing defensive football at your team's ground, are defending because that is all they are capable of, and anyway, they are being spoilsports.

Your cloggers are *hard tackling* and *tenacious*; their defenders are *dirty* and *crude*. Your team going for a long run without a win is going through a *re-building phase*; an opposition team going through a long run without a victory is *going over the hill*. Your team scoring against the run of play, is a matter of *brilliant* counter attacking; the opposition scoring against the run of play, is *goal grabbing*. When it comes to saving penalties, the opposition *miss* penalties, while in your team, the goalkeeper makes a *brilliant save*. When a ref, gives a hard decision against the opposition, he is being *firm and resolute*; when he gives a hard decision against your team, he is a *short sighted, idiotic little power maniac, who should get back to his sweetshop in Sussex double fast.*

Whatever sort of supporter you are, your first priority must always be getting to the ground in such a way as to avoid all trouble. This is quite easy, really, and just a little costly. If you are stupid enough to live near a ground, move out to the country. Never travel on public transport on Saturdays, or on Football Specials and always take care to travel to and from football matches in a sealed steel container.

Buy a phrase book for away matches, available in Scouse, Mancunian, Geordie, Brummy, Cockney and Yokel. If you are planning to attend football matches regularly (more fool, you), then a couple of vital extras are: the Coward's Coat, with reversible colours, which you can turn inside out when confronted with opposition fans. And the Shell Guide, with symbols, to Football Safety.

Where Not To Stand

When and if one gets to the ground, your troubles are by no means over. Where you stand, and what you shout out when you get there, are no small matters. The Shell Guide contains a list of all-purpose chants for cowards. As far as standing is concerned, it is advisable not to stand at the foot of the terraces, where you will end up knee deep in piss. There are other reasons, apart from cascading piss, why it is advisable not to stand at the front of terraced stands; here, you suffer from bottles, bricks, toilet rolls and referee-bound mothers-in-law.

It is not advisable to stand in the middle of football crowds; this is where the swaying and pushing happens; this is also where the pickpockets operate, another charming group of people eking out

a living on the fringes of football. And it is certainly not advisable to stand at the back of crowds; this is where toilet rolls, etc. are primed, to be thrown at the ref. and opposing supporters, and you could easily become part of the 'etc'.

Some people say it is best not to go at all, and to stay at home and watch the whole spectacle on television. But, as any true football supporter will tell you, by staying at home, you miss the atmosphere : the sound of breaking limbs and breathless bodies, the cascade of piss and blood, the roar of toilet rolls, the screams of abuse, the drooling of sociologists and the sweet sound of studs tearing into human flesh on the field, that almost forgotten part of the whole drama.

Some people, perhaps the same ones who stay at home and watch it all on television, speculate that perhaps football does not exist, and maybe, never existed, and it is all a big hoax dreamt up by the television people. Silly people. I am sure such things are not true.

One small safety precaution that will guarantee your immunity from police brutality, is to take a bag of oats for the police horses. When I have learned how to get your oats at football, I will pass that on, too.

Contrary to general opinion, there is not just one sort of football supporter, but many types. For a start, there are the Bovver Boys, who demanded a chapter of their own, or they would beat me up. They may be found in Chapter Eight. Then, there are little boys who come to pick pockets, learn how to be a hooligan, and stand at the front of the stand, shouting rude things at the other team's goalkeeper. Then there is that rare breed of supporter, the intellectual fan. They do rather silly things like writing poems about Mugsy, and talk to each other in very loud voices about the intellectual ramifications of Vincent's body swerve. They also talk, very seriously, about the 'Symbolism' of the game, and the hidden ambiguities of the 'Inverted System of Defence' (a snobbish way of describing the 'M System of Defence', itself a bit of a mystery).

Intellectual Supporters

Intellectual supporters, apart from the fact they are few and far between, and thus, excessively prominent, can be identified by their elderly duffle coats, and intense expressions worn throughout the match, when everyone else is shouting, singing, changing, fighting, stabbing and breaking bottles over other people's heads.

To become this sort of supporter, you need a duffle coat, very intellectual-looking spectacles, scruffy hair, a high-pitched voice, the ability to maintain the most intensely clever argument for several hours about the most boring of teams, and the ability to say witty things about the referee. It is really impossible to bluff your way into being a supporter of this variety; you either are one or you are not. Most of us, fortunately, are not.

The handful of intellectual supporters attached to each club stand in deadly earnest little groups, wearing their team's rosettes, clutching cups of steaming tea at the entrance to the terraces. They are somewhat afraid to venture straight into the actual terraces, where Bovver Boys are conducting an altogether different sort of dialogue.

Surprisingly, the intellectuals are some of the most fanatical and bigoted of supporters. When the defence gets in a tangle, they are to be heard shouting above the rest of the crowd : "For God's sake, Jock, give it to Robby !" and "Don't mess about Masher, get it out to O'Guiness !" The sight and sound of such cultured bigots is the one thing always guaranteed to stop Bovver Boys in their tracks, as they look on in amazement. "I say ref, are you blind as well as stupid?" "Superb play Crushers, superb play !"

Distinguished Visitors

There are many types of football fan unknown to the ordinary and rather stupid man on the terraces. At almost every English Football League home game, there are a horde of foreign dignitaries who have asked to see this "Football" they have heard so much about. At any time during the season, a club's Visitors' enclosure is likely to be choc-a-bloc with the Nig of Nog and the Tik of Tok and representatives of the South Pacific Islands' Football Federation, on a fact-finding mission to discover this 'Glorious Religion of Football' they have all heard about. Several visiting delegations of cannibals have shown interest in taking Mugsy back and making him a God and part of their traditional rites.

The Japanese Project

A special section of the seating is always reserved for Japanese businessmen, who have been studying the football phenomenon with a view to producing an imitation of the game back home in Japan, at a quarter of the cost. They sit crouched over burgeoning notebooks, taking meticulous notes of every tackle and clog. They estimate that they can produce the world's first automated, clockwork clogging Full Back in three years. In the event of failing to meet that deadline, they will execute everybody concerned in the project, and offer 2,200 transistor radios for Sid Scythe. A 3 ft. 6 in. Japanese cameraman sprints up and down the touchline, taking ground views of some of the more horrendous tackles, for detailed study later.

Old Men Remember

Another type of supporter is The Croaker. This fan has to be at least 90, and preferably, bad tempered and irritable. Every Football Club has a Croakers' Enclosure, the place where all the old men who know it all, sit through the game croaking about how bad this and that is, and how very much better the game was in the old days. And of course : "They don't make footballers like that any more".

Croakers always leave the match 20 minutes from the end, muttering in disgust, and beat up other teams' Croakers who have left similarly early. This is a good way of getting their Bovver over before the real thugs get stuck in.

The younger supporters find the Croakers very irritating. In fact, anybody under 107 finds the Croakers very irritating. So it becomes necessary to place the Croakers far out of toilet roll reach from the ordinary terraces. It was for this purpose that Cantilever, Double and Treble Decker Stands were invented.

This way, the Croakers while placed way up at the top of the huge stand, can still retain a bird's eye view of the loathsome action. If you hear a constant background grumbling mumble from the general direction of the clouds, you know that your Club's very own Croakers' Enclosure is in full swing at the top of their canti-lever stand. And to confirm the point, elderly circa 1933 toilet rolls sometimes work their way on to the pitch.

Celebrated Supporters

Another group of deeply concerned outsiders who earnestly seek to contribute their talents to the game they so love, is made up of various social celebrities. Hardly a day goes by without a film star, pop singer or television personality, aligning himself with a parti-cular Football Club. Also, hopefully, aligning himself with a life-long free season ticket at the same Club and permanent social access to the Big Names therein.

Ham United are fortunate enough to have the unflinching loyalty of Miss Sally Anne Floozy, the internationally famous Cabaret Artiste and Society Hostess of unlimited dimensions. And also of Mr. Bernard Bilge, renowned pavement artist and scrap metal dealer, of 24 The Buildings, Deptford, Southwark. These, and other internationally celebrated personalities, have an open invitation to visit the club's dressing rooms whenever there is a home game, if they are passing through London at the time. Miss Floozy says her knowledge of football has increased vastly since she has paid several visits to the Ham United dressing rooms. Miss Lulu Charmers, the popular strip artiste and film star, claims she is a fan not only of Ham United, but of football in general. This perhaps explains her open, standing invitation to the dressing rooms of every football club in the country.

Another celebrated fan of the team, and any other team that accepts him, is Alexander Tootsywoots, the well-known fashion designer, and one of the eager designers of Jock Straps referred to in Chapter Three. Alexander takes his place with the chorus of swooning poofs who never miss a home game, and bring their own tender lavender cushions to sit on, ". . . seats are so hard, don't you think, ducky?" An endless succession of "ooohs" and "aaahs" accom-pany every physical manoeuvre on the pitch, emanating from this

HAM UTD.
WELCOME TO
THIS WEEKS
CELEBRITY!

section of the crowd, rising to a shrieking crescendo when the trainer sprints out on to the pitch to massage a fallen player's wounded parts.

Such stars are given seats in the Celebrities' Enclosure, which is discreetly distanced from the Wives' enclosure, which is discreetly distanced from the Groupies' enclosure. And all such enclosures, of course, are situated well away from the actual football fans on the terraces. Scientists tell us that in ten years' time, ordinary fans on the terraces will be the smallest group of people attending football matches. The ground will be divided between Social Celebrities, Psychiatrists, Sociologists, Directors, Chairmen, Agents, Groupies and Bovver Boys. And ordinary fans who just want to go along to watch a football match will have to submit their reasons in writing ten days in advance, and be issued with special passes.

Long Term Prospects

Ham United have commissioned a special report on the long term prospects of the game, and what shape the club will be in ten years' time. This report predicted that the club would be in a healthy state if Chairman Knowlesworth-Blair stopped taking money out of the club and using it as a vehicle for his personal prestige. So this report was suppressed, and another one commissioned. This second report said Ham United would soon become a minor subsidiary of Knowlesworth Breweries, and that the footballers' training facilities in the ground would be reduced to an absolute minimum. Several of the stands would be turned into sorely needed community projects such as a £3½ million Bovverama, to deal with the social problems of disaffected youth. (This projected facility to include a strangling centre for bored and frustrated youths, who at any time they feel the need, could walk in and strangle the first adult they set eyes on.)

The club's gymnasiums, the report predicts, will be turned into consulting rooms for Psychiatrists and Sociologists, analysing depressed fans, while the rest of the ground will be turned into warehouses for Knowlesworth products, and offices for the staff of Consolidated Conmen of Lewisham.

Ideas For Entry

In the meantime, people will do anything to get into a football ground free. No Christmas cracker is complete without a suggested wheeze to get into a football ground on the sly. Some people claim that they have come to polish the floodlights, or cut the grass (just before kick off!). More daring chaps arrive at the players' entrance with bags of football kit, saying they have brought it for So-and-So, who left it behind in his rush to get to the ground. They wish to get down to the changing rooms to hand over the kit.

Clubs usually reply to such attempts: "Yes, thank you very much", take the kit, and turn the trickster away. Several clubs are known to equip their entire first team squad this way.

Some unscrupulous people try to wheeze their way free into football grounds by saying that they are doing research for silly Handbooks about Football. The game is being brought gravely into disrepute when such things happen.

It is not at all uncommon for a host of 'Electricians' to descend on the ground on match days. They all have highly creditable stories such as that they have come to mend the plug in the Manager's office, or the wiring in the floodlights needs adjusting that afternoon.

If you are a policeman, it is slightly easier, of course. You can apply to become one of the thousands of policemen detailed to do Bovver Duty every Saturday afternoon. Policemen can put their names down on the Bovver Rota, and thus get to see a free home game once a month or so. In fact, many far-sighted football fans join the Police with this in mind, only to find that they are posted to a station in South Cornwall or the Highlands of Scotland, or some such uncivilised non-football area. When the local club is going through a bad phase, or is itself just plain bad, things have to be organised differently. When Ham United had their all-time low four seasons ago, Saturday afternoon at Ham United was detailed as Punishment Duty at the local 'nick'.

You Could Of Course Pay

If, however, you aspire to be that rarity in soccer, the ordinary fan who goes to matches because he likes football, your task is quite simple, and you do not have to spend a lifetime becoming a Policeman, Celebrity, Groupie, Agent, Poof, Croaker or Bovver Boy. Simply, every Saturday afternoon, take your normal place on the terraces, next to the Sociologist studying crowd behaviour, and behind the Sociologist observing the implications of the game on the field. On the other side of the barrier will be a Sociologist studying the effect of crowd behaviour on the players, in front of a plain clothes Policeman, and beside a couple of chappies from the University armed with clipboards doing their thesis on football. All of these are surrounded by Freddy Terror's Lawyers and Solicitors, waiting to pounce on the Police as they eject the leader of the Skull End from the ground for the 314th time that season. This may be regarded as a typical bit of terrace on any English Football Ground on any Saturday afternoon at any time throughout the season.

CHAPTER EIGHT

How To Be A Bovver Boy

> *Parents! Buy this new great game that will keep your children quiet for hours! Great free Bovver Boots competition. Will keep them amused for days on end! Just get them to send in their old steel combs, knuckle dusters, and sawn off shotguns, and back will come a brand new, shining, ready for action, pair of Bovver Boots! They will love them! Just sit back and watch the little darlings put the boot into everyone in sight, and make lots of new friends as they meet other little boys with this marvellous football souvenir. Banish Boredom with Blood!! Send orders to Rentathug, Knuckle House, Brute Way, Savage, Cheshire.*

EVERY season has its Football Hooligan period; this is the time when the football gets especially dull and defensive, the papers get tired of reporting the same players kicking each other week in and out, and an unusually large number of Magistrates go coco in their denunciations of modern youth and society.

Food For Correspondence

It is the time of the season when Managers express their deeply felt shock at this intrusion of violence into the game. And it is the period when players take time off from kicking the hell out of each other to instruct their ghost writers to insert a bit in their column in the papers saying, "All this unnecessary violence is bringing our game into disrepute. Why don't they go and play football instead?"

It is one of the many times of year when batteries of indignant retired Colonels take pen to paper to write to *The Times* about "This Menace that Must Be Stamped Out!"

> *"Surely the time has come for all right thinking citizens to rally round and state clearly that the time has come to put a stop to the meagre, soft hearted, half measures of the*

> *lily livered authorities, too timid to take the measures*
> *which are clearly necessary if decent living people are to*
> *continue to enjoy the peace and security that is the birth-*
> *right of every living Englishman. And every dead one,*
> *too."*

It is said by some that these Colonels keep piles of such written letters close at hand, to be dispatched to the Editor of *The Times* at the first sight of any relevant event. These people also allege that football hooliganism was invented solely for the benefit of these retired Colonels, so as to give them an appropriate subject on which to vent their indignation throughout old age. I am sure such accusations are quite untrue, and even if they are true, they certainly have no place in a dignified Handbook about Football like this one.

However, this is to anticipate our guide to football hooliganism, and how you, the uninvolved innocent, may become a raging thug on Saturday afternoons. Football hooliganism has been an integral part of football for as long as anyone can remember; indeed, there have been hooligans in football even longer than there have been Sociologists. Which shows you just how old the tradition of football hooliganism must be.

The phenomenon as it stands in modern days is a delight for the research-hungry Sociologist, or Colour Supplement Plebian Sniffer. Every Saturday afternoon, tens of thousands of shaven headed, armour plated, boot brandishing, bowler hatted, teeth gnashing, snarling youths descend on the football grounds of this country, to beat the hell out of each other, and sometimes innocent spectators as well. Then they depart, sometimes long before the actual football game has started. Although they do occasionally pause on their way out of the ground, to sing insults at the teams as they come out of the tunnel, and any opposition supporters who have been stupid enough to turn up.

These are the Bovver Boys—the backbone of our modern youth, the flower of our nation, the inheritors of our civilisation, our rulers of tomorrow. (Or at least, so said one of the few Sociologists who got back alive to report the result of his studies. Whether his opinions would have been shared by the thousands of his colleagues trampled under boot in their valiant efforts to record the life style of Skinheads, is another matter.)

Football Hooliganism is a natural phase through which most young men pass. It can be regarded as merely one of a number of transitory phases such as tree strangling, teacher asphyxiating, cannibalism, parent mugging, and pet impaling that any normal healthy young adolescent goes through at some time or another.

A Passing Phase

Horrified parents who whip their sons off to Psychiatrists at the first sign of hooliganism—usually around nine years old these days —with the youngster in question disrupting the game in his local park, are always told there is nothing to worry about, that little Johnny will soon grow out of it, that it is a necessary outlet for his emotions and frustrated instincts. Little Johnny then breaks a bottle over the Psychiatrist's head, and the session comes to an abrupt end.

For a definitive opinion on the nature of the football hooligan, I turned to the well known Sociologist, Dr. A. S. Quak, of Quak, Quak, Quak and Quak, Sociologists. Mr. Quak told me: "It is quite easy to detect the lad who later in life is to become a Social Malcontent, or, as society deems to call them, Football Hooligans. He is the lad who, when told he cannot play with his little brother's toy soldiers, decapitates them all, and throws the heads on the fire; he is the young lad who goes round stabbing people who will not give him a penny for the Guy in November. He will most likely be the lad who hurls furniture across the room, rapes his teacher and sets light to the building, on his first day in primary school. He is a youngster who has found the precepts of modern society to be inadequate and wanting. His alienation, for it is nothing less, springs from his deep and utter dissatisfaction with the values and mores of modern society.

"I would say that however horrible society deems these things to be, we should in no way punish him for his misbehaviour, or in any way make him feel rejected because of our hostility. We should not put up barriers against these deprived lads. Every effort should be made to integrate them into the community, even when this means they will smash it up. It is vital that we do not lessen their creative potential for later in life, that we do not disturb the delicate balance of their sensitivity. They must have every chance to work out their frustrations and energies, with the minimum of interference from authority". Dr. Quak, it may be added, has never met a hooligan in his life, and would not know a Bovver Boot if he saw one, which is extremely unlikely, because he never leaves his consulting rooms in Hampstead.

Hard Hearted Magistrates

Magistrates, on the other hand, are over-hard on football hooligans. The resident Justice of the Peace for the Ham United area is Mr. Henry Whistleworth-Blair, a portly wealthy gentleman, who is not wholly unrelated to Chairman Knowlesworth-Blair of Ham United, and whose business is not wholly disconnected with the Ham United Ground. This, if one was nasty and mean minded enough to make such suggestions, could account for his embittered reaction to all football hooligans brought before his bench, and some of his horrific sentences. Horrific even by loony JP standards.

Justice Whistleworth-Blair holds special sessions on Monday mornings, taking an extended break from his arduous duties as Chairman of Blair, Blare, Blare and Blair Limited, to deal with the hundreds of hooligans who have been apprehended the previous Saturday. The Mondays after reserve games are not so bad; reserve games are attended by apprentice hooligans when they first want

to try out being hooligans. It is usually a matter of hordes of 11-year-olds battering each other with rolled up newspapers and soft drink cartons, with the occasional paving stone thrown in for good measure, to develop muscles for the real thing later on. The little horrors then rush off to meet the real homecoming hooligans, on their battered Special Train, to report their progress in terror that day.

But Monday mornings at Justice Blair's after a Saturday First Team home game, are an altogether different matter. Not for nothing are these sessions known locally as the Hanging Hours. The sessions take extraordinarily long, because the Judge invariably spends hours haranguing the first case, and his parents, as well as any Social Workers and Psychiatrists who have been unwise enough to come along to speak in his defence.

The Same Old Record

The Judge, in his long winded outbursts, is not unlike the footballers themselves, with their stock phrases for television, and word training. Except that he perms his oratory from : "The youth of today does not know what is good for them." "When I was a boy, we never had any of this nonsense." "These people today do not know the meaning of the word discipline." "We should never have abolished the Cat/Whip/Birch/Hanging/Flogging/Head Chopping/Torture". (Select one, depending on the degree of his hangover from the previous night's drinking at his Club.) And of course, everybody's Golden Oldie : "They ought never to have abolished National Service. What you chaps need is a spell in the Army".

All cases are found guilty, and given the maximum possible sentence. After this, the Judge then harangues those present about the mildness of the sentence he is allowed to hand out, and how he fears for the future of the country when the maximum sentence he is allowed to impose on a 17-year-old hooligan for his first offence is a £100 fine and three years in Borstal.

A Spell Inside

After sentencing, all Skinheads are sent to special Skinhead prisoner-of-war camps, where, upon meeting each other and rubbing crops together, they learn to be even nastier than before. Here, in the prison camps, the wise authorities divert the Skinheads' aggressive intentions with basketwork, floor scrubbing and art classes. Then, before he leaves, each Skinhead is asked to cross his heart and promise that he will not be naughty again, and is set loose on a petrified world. Now, clambering past the applauding ranks of Social Workers, Sociologists, Psychiatrists, and general Do-Gooders who think that Skinheads are really ever such nice people, if only they were given a chance, he goes back to try and find his mates who are not inside, to start all over again.

A Soft Touch

Judges vary around the country, although Justice Blair is fairly typical of a large number of them. But some Judges are well known to be a soft touch, and are amenable to the weakest line in sob stories. And bearing this in mind, the bright hooligan picks his spot for a bit of bovver very carefully.

It is from these cases that one hears all the "I never meant it" and "I don't know what came over me" type of stories. One hooligan, asked what he was doing with a collection of 300 knives in the back of his van while travelling to an away match, said, "I collect 'em, don't I?" These also tend to be the courts where all the defendants appear to have ageing, sick parents whom they must stay with, and look after, or else they will take a turn for the worse. Other soft explanations generally accepted by soft Judges, include for stabbing, "My hand slipped"; for breaking a milk bottle over someone's head, "I was just taking them bottles back to the dairy, when I slipped".

It was the endless chain of incidents like these that led to the formation of the by now famous Committee to Investigate Football Hooliganism. The move to set up the committee was sparked off by an incident that shook the football world to its very studs. A group of hooligans ran on to the pitch in a Second Division game and beat up the referee—*after* he had already been beaten up by the players!! The need for some sort of action to stop such things happening again, was obvious. As one well-known Centre Half put it, "We can't have them doing our work for us, can we? I'd be out of a job in a fortnight if this sort of thing kept happening". A further damning indictment of such mindless hooliganism was provided by Mugsy, turning from his 13th telephone directory that morning, "I mean, it ain't rite is it, all this violence? It's all bad for the image of the game, innit?"

A Cross Section

The Committee was set up to investigate the increased wave of football hooliganism, its origins, and what could be done to stamp it out. The government took great care to select a representative cross section of opinion to the Committee. As well as ensuring that it was made up of people whose knowledge of football, and attachment to the game was wholly apparent, great efforts were made to ensure that the younger generation would not feel that the Committe was out of touch with modern youth.

The Committee was composed of Lady Cynthia Bradleysnot, 87, a nice lady with lots of money who lives in Kensington and does things for poor people; the well-known singer and cabaret artist, Jim Burpalong, who had three Number One hits in the 1930's; Sir Horace Brevington Smythe, OBE, Knight of the Knickers and well-known lecher; Mr. Blank of Boring, Sussex, a very dull retired Civil Servant, who was selected to represent the opinions of very dull retired civil servants; the Bishop of Muggingthorpe, The Right Reverend Cuthbert Snooze; and Lord Littlesense of Feudal, Gloucestershire. These Committees always like to have a Lord on them, to make them look important.

To ensure that the Committee at all times remained in touch with the younger generation, the transcripts of all proceedings were handed on to an 11-year-old schoolboy from Hampshire, Oliver Squeek, who had won a School Composition Prize for his essay on "What is wrong with the world, and what I would do to put it right".

Interview

The Committee interviewed a wide ranging consensus of concerned people in its inquiry. It interviewed JPs, Detention Centre Warders, retired Majors, retired Colonels, Vicars, Social Workers, people who had been killed by hooligans, frustrated Hangmen and Noose Manufacturers, indignant people who had written to the papers complaining about hooliganism, as well as the usual cross section of Psychologists, Psychiatrists and Sociologists. To give the Report an aura of balance, an interview with a hooligan was rushed into the Appendix.

The Report

After its 11-month inquiry, the Committee produced a 7,000 word document, which was proclaimed as the most successful attempt yet at producing a long winded and boring document on a simple subject. A special paperback edition was produced for hooligans, written in grunt language, by Boot Press, Kick-On-The-Oooglees, Staffs.

Among the Committee's recommendations were that football should be abolished and be replaced by officially supervised massacres, kill-ins and small local wars. The Committee recommended that failing this, all football matches should be licensed with a U or A Certificate, according to the amount of violence on the field and terrace. Most matches would have to have an X Certificate, it was realised. They further suggested that children under 25 should not be admitted to football matches unless accompanied by a parent, and only then if they had done all their homework for the week.

As an interim measure, the Committee suggested that a three months' amnesty be held for football hooligans to give those with a troubled conscience a chance to reform. During this period, any hooligan could go into his local police station and hand over any poisoned darts, Mills bombs, or thermic lances with a guarantee of immunity. After this, a further three months' amnesty to be held for hooligans who did not know what 'amnesty' or 'immunity' meant, during which any hooligan surrendering his boots at his local station would be given a papiermâché boot in the colours of his team.

The report was sent to the Minister of Sport, and was last seen making its 35th journey down Whitehall in a taxi, in search of that personage.

A New Police Policy

In their ceaseless efforts to stamp out hooliganism, the Police have from time to time increased the squads of plain clothes Policemen from their ranks. The regulation size 15 polished shoes, boring grey mac worn whatever the weather, and the fact that they did not join in some of the more delightful Skull End ditties, soon gave them away. So a policy of subterfuge had to be invented to achieve the original purpose. The policy of subterfuge failed because the average Policeman did not know what a big word like 'subterfuge' meant. So the policy was re-named the "Operation For Dressing Up As Hooligans So That The Hooligans Will Not Recognise Us When We Go Among Them On Match Days At 15.00 Hours Sharp". This time the scheme met with some limited success. Which meant that the plain clothes Police were not recognised, but were repeatedly arrested by uniformed Police, clearing up spots of Bovver.

Hooligans who are thrown out of the crowd are led outside, told to not do it again, and set free. They then, of course, promptly pay again at the turnstiles, and come back and hooliganise again. That is except for the hooligans who commit the most heinous offences; they are put in the cells to await Judge Blair's wrath on Monday.

A Way To Raise Money

Letting the hooligans loose, so that they can come straight back in again, is not an accidental aspect of club policy. Director Smith Jones keeps a careful eye on the books, and when he spots any club debts accruing, he tells the Chief Hooligan Prevention Officer, how many Bovver Boys he wants thrown out that week to achieve the necessary increased number of 50p's.

The Gear

Bovver Boys, as any Sociologist will tell you, are most particular about their appearance; the well dressed hooligan this season, for example, is wearing a tapered bullet proof vest, and would not be seen dead in anything less. Hooligan fashions for the season are very important; if you are wearing *last* season's gear or carrying a weapon from last season, you can get battered to death, or even worse, shunned by your fellow hooligans.

Fashion shows for hooligans are held just prior to the season in desolate warehouses and cemeteries; prospective modes of dress and also of things to wear, are modelled by appropriately vicious models, and a consensus of opinion sought. They also ask you what you fink. Votes on the various systems of apparel are taken by a show of sharpened steel combs, and the volume of grunts emanating from the floor where the hooligans are sitting because they broke all the available makeshift furniture over each other's heads before the proceedings started.

New Weapons

There are very definite trends in hooligan fashion and life style that can easily be missed by the casual sociologist; last year, for instance, Thermonuclear devices were *in*, and ordinary tactical nuclear weapons were very much out. This year, however, no self respecting hooligan would be seen dead, or even alive, with a Thermonuclear; it has just got to be a tactical nuclear weapon.

Part of the reason for the change is that since last season, when two Policemen's helmets were lost due to hooliganism, the Police have been especially vigorous in their anti-hooligan campaign, and have been stopping and searching hooligans at the turnstiles. Last season 347 people were massacred by hooligans, an increase of 17 on the previous season's total, but the Chief Constable of England and Wales said he thought this was not sufficient reason for "any degree of public alarm". "One has to accept these things, harsh as they may seem, as part of the hazards of everyday life." But stealing Policemen's helmets is something else.

The Smaller The Better

A Thermonuclear weapon, as those of you who are hooligans or nuclear scientists will know, is rather bulky and quite impossible to conceal under an overcoat. Tactical nuclear weapons come in much smaller sizes, and can be slipped into the top of a boot at the first sign of 'Law and Order'.

In spite of these rather anti-social aspects of football hooliganism,

one should not ignore its beneficial social implications. It is, for example, a blessing to spare-part surgery. Any doctor in need of a spare part may find a veritable feast of spares on a terrace, after a game is finished. Here can be found arms, hands, legs, fingers, skulls, all for nothing. Not to mention countless pints of blood, from all blood groups, kindly donated by stabbed victims.

Football hooliganism also gives employment to countless thousands of Psychologists, Psychiatrists and Do-Gooders of every variety. Such people might otherwise have to starve, or cke out a career analysing the headhunters of New Guinea, themselves already overwhelmed with head-shrinking Psychologists. In fact, one must mention here, in an absolutely irrelevant aside, that to do a sociological survey of the latest tribe of New Guinea headhunters, or make a TV documentary about their imminent demise at the hands of the white man's civilisation, due to disease transmitted by hordes of snooping outsiders, one has to arrange a booking with their London agents. This has not yet happened with football hooligans, although Freddy Terror's lawyers are working on it. Snarling hooligans can, of course, be provided to order, for TV panel games, by Rent-a-Thug, Lewisham, London.

CHAPTER NINE

How To Win The Cup

Great Cup Competition!!! To win your free plastic, replica Cup, send 15 vouchers from the corner of The Football Handbook To End All Football Handbooks, *along with the names of the last 43 winners of the FA Cup, and lots of money, to: Ripoff Enterprises, The Derelict House On The Corner, Cheat Street, Scunthorpe (or just send lots of money).*

THE CUP was invented by Psychologists, anxious to counteract the tedium of ordinary League Football, and prevent non-League sides, who also participate in the Cup, from developing an inferiority complex about their lowly situation. Also, they calculated that if the Cup Final were to be held at Wembley and made the climax of the season, this would give rise to the certified parasites' paradise of Cup Final Day which, in turn, would provide an unparalleled opportunity for Sociological study.

Last year, Ham United won the Cup. Before this, they had gone six years without winning anything. Some folks say this is because they had no players of real ability during this period; others say that they had plenty of players with ability, but not enough Cloggers. Others say that the lack of success was because they had lost the subtle art of bribery. Others say that they went without success for so long because they were such a bloody awful side.

In last year's competition, they struggled long and hard with the mighty amateurs of Brimble Town, the game going to six replays before Ham United could bring themselves to score a goal and get rid of the infuriating butchers and bakers who had shown themselves every bit as good as Ham United's overpaid flash lads. After several nondescript victories in the intervening rounds, they went on to subdue the reigning League Champions, Plymouth Muggers, in the Semi-Final, before finally staggering, knackered, up the famous Empire Way at Wembley for the Final. Only to find that they had got the date wrong.

A Sense Of Direction

One of the purposes of the Cup is to have big Clubs like Ham United drawn away to idiotic and rather silly places like Barnsley and Walton-on-the-Naze, thus giving the Skull End a chance to sack a totally new town, and give Mugsy a chance to kick a different breed of player. As most of you know, the FA Cup was the cause of geography being taught in schools. If Bovver Boys were going to go off sacking and pillaging the more remote corners of the country, every time the Cup came around, it was thought best that they should be given a sense of direction to help them on their way.

Villagers' Reaction

The Third Round of the Cup is a great day in the English sporting calendar. This year, Ham United have been drawn away to Grimble Town, a small Gloucestershire village (population 218, including substitutes), for the Third Round. All the villagers are thrilled, and are looking forward to seeing the famous Ham United players, who up until now have only been names in the newspapers, faces on the television when they have been sent off on Match of the Day, and on bits of plastic in a cereal packet. They are also looking forward to meeting all the 28,000 travelling Ham United fans, renowned everywhere for their sportsmanship and appreciation of fair play, or at least, so the local 'Clarion' has been telling its readers. Poor fools! They will soon know the truth . . .

The local undertaker, Ebenezer Grinswalde, is shrewder. He has laid in extra stock for the weekend.

More typical of the townsfolk's reactions is that of the Vicar, who is leading Thanksgiving Services in his church, for this timely visit by a leading Football League club. This will do much to uplift the spirit of the people of Grimble Town, and the bank balance of their football club. Grimble Town, like Ham United, have seen the wisdom of investing in a good Reverend on the Board.

The vicar is a very distant and unimportant relative of the Reverend Carlesworth A. Bore. The Reverend Bore tries to avoid him at all costs. "Such a common fellow" he says. The Reverend Bore is very embarrassed by the Cup draw.

The village Policeman spends the week before the match polishing his bicycle, in anticipation of the extra duties.

Sharpened Knives

Meanwhile, in Intimidation Terrace, the sound of knives being sharpened can be heard clearly above the sound of the night's muggings, and there are cries of "Where's this Grimble place, then?" Elderly Bovver Boys are consulted as to the whereabouts of Grimble, and the likelihood of a good fight there.

British Rail are also trying hard to locate the town, and check whether they have a line running to the place. If they have, the hunt will be on to find old stock, bad and derelict enough for the hooligans of Ham United to wreck.

Fleet Street reporters reluctantly worm their way down to the West Country, barricade themselves firmly in the Rose and Crown when they arrive for the duration of the whole damn silly affair, and set about finding a silly 70-year-old rustic who will say senile things like, "We is going to whip them city slickers rite good and proper".

One Who Knows

One of the few people who views the coming influx of homely Cockneys with something less than joy is the village ex-Cockney cab driver, Syd Smart. He made his fortune in London some years ago, and then scarpered, before any questions could be asked. He knows what is coming. He has taken his wife, kids and worldly possessions into hiding in the hills for the weekend.

Contrary to Fleet Street scepticism, the exercise does have several purposes. For a start, it gives the Bovver Boys a bit of variety in their Bovver, and a new town to ransack. Psychologists have told us that it is very damaging to a boy's ego if he has to ransack the same football grounds, week in and out. And, of course, it gives Mugsy and like-minded sadists new faces to kick.

The Chairman travels on the Friday before the game, on a reconnaissance for cheap labour for his lumber mills. While Director Smith-Jones travels in the middle of the previous week, to make a quick tour of the town and urge villagers to ensure their property, lives and livestock against the imminent invasion of thousands of short-tempered, brawling, nasty Londoners. He finds this technique never fails.

The local paper in Grimble is rushing out a special issue with faded pictures and misprints, for the occasion. It contains a rustic guide to Grimble Town FC, for the information of the inhabitants of the village who have never even heard of it until the Cup draw.

They're Here

At last, the Great Day arrives. At 12.00 Grimble Town Time, the 20 Zoo Specials arrive from London, having had their communication cords pulled a mere 28 times—far below normal excursion standards. From this it may be surmised that the Skull End are eager to get down to the West Country and start pillaging unknown regions.

The remainder of the day follows the traditional form of these one-sided contests. Thousands of beer-crazed Cockneys descend on the town, locating the Village Whore, Public House and Football Ground, in that order, and leave each in a suitably devastated state. Many ransack the solitary pub, and steal the club's floodlights for a souvenir, before climbing back on to the returning Special, completely forgetting why they came down in the first place. While other supporters find the rustic charms of Grimbleshire quite over-whelming, decide to settle there for good, and turn their backs on the grim big-city life, until at least the next home game.

Just Desserts

Others descend on the nearest haystacks, and start tearing them down with their bare hands, in the hope of discovering some truth in the legends about local lasses who frolic in haystacks. They usually end up discovering some truths about the sharpness of Yokel pitchforks, instead. Other equally unfortunate city lads, in a state of advanced inebriation, attempt to engage the locals in conversation in a fruitless attempt to reach the match. Such attempts at communication usually end up with the visitors being directed into Farmer Jones' Manure Store, or, as often as not, the shotgun that he keeps poised for all such intruders. Many a harmless young hooligan coming down to wile away his time with a bit of pillage and plunder, has ended up spending the rest of his life, chained to a team of Oxen, pulling a plough from dawn to dusk.

And, if one dare say it, there are countless examples of lads who came down to these rural venues seeking a bit of the other, and ended up working on the udders.

However, for the sober, upright, God-fearing majority of football fans who are able to make their way straight to the ground, resisting the temptations of crumpet, booze, massacre and general all-round pillage, there is the game of football, the original cause of these horrendous manifestations which the Chairman will have to dissociate the club from in the programme for the next home game.

The football is to be found at the Grimble Town Football and Athletic Ground, which also doubles as the Grimble Town Race Course, Market and Golf Course. Here, under ancient shuddering floodlights, creaking grandstands and on a pitch potmarked with craters, the humble little footballers of Grimble Town will attempt to intimidate men to whom the thud of a stud on flesh, is sweet music. (Thank you, Sid Hack of the *Daily Splurge*, third table along, Rose and Crown, for that last line. Such a pity you could not make the match.)

Pitchforks Rattle

The truth about these affairs is that the actual match is always an anti-climax. The big team always wins, although the papers run routine headlines about "Heroic Cup Minnows", "Brave Little Battlers of Grimble Town" and "Underdogs Go Down Fighting". The cynicism of newspapers being what it is, such headlines are set before the actual match has taken place. Still, the result is small beer to the cheering yokels, beside themselves with cider, as their next-door-neighbours chop down Europe's finest in full flight. In this particular match—a tremendous embarrassment to Manager

Jock and all concerned—the Yokels make their presence felt by the rattling of pitchforks every time their colleagues cross the half-way line. Those members of the Skull End not comatose in the pub, or incarcerated in the nick, are fascinated by the pitchforks—the going rate at Grimble was one pitchfork for four steel combs and a pair of braces.

Interest is also shown in combine harvesters and threshing machines, but none of the Skull End present could muster the required 20,000 steel combs or 11,000 silver chrome Bovver Boots. Diamond 'Anybody's' Lil, of 414 Dagenham Road, Dockside, was offered in part exchange along with a Vincent Silk Scarf, and negotiations were entered into on that basis.

Victory

Grimble Town were disposed of to the tune of 6–0, and the Reverend Bore stayed on to conduct a Service for those of the villagers massacred on the Saturday. "The least we could do," said Chairman Knowlesworth-Blair, who returned hotfoot to London, before the match, when he found the pub did not serve Six Star Brandy.

In spite of the abrupt exit of the silly little teams, such fixtures do serve several useful purposes. Such Cup Ties breathe a wind of excitement into the lives of rustic country Magistrates, who have long since nodded off with only the occasional case of apple-scrumping to adjudicate. It can be quite a shock suddenly to have to deal with 500 ferocious Cockney hooligans, whose history of court appearances makes them a match for any examining Magistrate or Lawyer in the country.

Aftermath

The result is often a vociferous over-reaction on the part of the Judge, who gleefully uses the maximum sentence at his disposal, usually denied him by the placidness of the local criminal populace.

Grimbleshire is a part of the country that still harbours warm memories of Hanging Judge Jeffries, and the local Magistrate is often barely restrained by wiser counsels from sentencing all before him to a lifetime's penal servitude in Botany Bay. In the face of such barbaric Law Makers, squads of sob story Sociologists and soft Social Workers rush down from London specially to plead the boys' cases. This has become standard practice in fact, and a flying squad of sob-story Sociologists, Social Workers and Do-Gooders is retained on call in London and all major cities, ready to be rushed anywhere in the country at the news of the first football offences arrests of the day. The end of the day's fighting and the beginning of the legal retributions, brings to the surface a scurrying plethora of soft-hearted nosy nincompoops, who would be terrified to raise their heads during the hour and a half after kick off time.

Away From It All

Whenever a big Cup Tie is approaching, Managers like to take their players 'away from it all', to the peace and quiet of an out-of-season holiday resort or remote hilltop training camp. They do this so as to remove all the distractions and temptations offered to footballers whilst in towns. Instead, at their remote hilltop training camp, they come into contact with remote hilltop groupies, remote hilltop pubs and remote hilltop night clubs. Resorts are really no better, because they keep bumping into groups of other footballers who have gone there to get away from it all. Many a crucial Cup Tie has been settled days before the actual game, on the blood stained beaches of the South Coast.

A Manager's Lot Is Not A Happy One

The strain on any Manager is equally great, and very often misunderstood. The Manager lives under permanent threat of wrath from the Chairman, or the learned displeasure of the Board as a whole. Whilst a Contract is a meaningless scrap of paper that offers him no protection, even if he could read it. This, plus his hatred/jealousy of his players, brings a Manager, regardless of his standing, into a rare unity of human feeling with all other Managers that so rarely passes across the face of our quarrelsome lives.

At seedy seaside resorts at Cup time, whilst the players roam the seafront grabbing bathing beauties and getting thrashed at beach football by the local truants, Managers sit in nervously aggressive insular huddles in their clammy hotels, peering over their shoulders as they compare Chairmen and Boards of Directors.

The pride of the Managers' group at the Fisherman's Arms in Knee-on-See last year was Tom McSteel, Manager of Scunthorpe Stabbers who had a guaranteed contract, with the option of suicide or public disembowelment, if the team lost more than three matches on the run. Low whispers of amazement ran around the lobby as he recited the terms of his contract. Very few Managers are given a *choice* in these matters—it was not even mandatory that he should have to commit suicide in front of the club's supporters.

It is not very widely known that the Japanese tradition of suicide, Hari Kari, has its origins in English Football. The act is named after Mr. Harry Karry, Manager of Wearyside Wanderers, who was the first Football Manager to publicly commit suicide when faced with the disgrace of dropping a point at home. Up until then, the practice had been for the unfortunate man to be beheaded in the team's gym, in front of the cheering first team squad and for his head then to be added to the practice balls used by the apprentices. However, Harry, who had a sense of community responsibility, felt that the Manager had let down not only his Chairman and the Board, but the public as well. He therefore committed suicide, falling on top of the Match ball for that afternoon, in the centre circle at kick-off time in a League Match. The Japanese businessmen who were present, taking note of the clogging techniques for incorporation into the eventual super-efficient Japanese model, were most impressed and passed word of this intriguing English custom back to their superiors.

Since then, things have gradually got better for the beleaguered Managers. While there are still some clubs that insist on hanging for the loss of two consecutive home games, the majority are far more broadminded. Most Chairman are content if the Manager volunteers to jump off the Main Stand with a football tied around his neck. If the defeats are the fault of the defence, he may be asked to jump off the Main Stand with the Centre Half around his neck. Alternatively, he may be let off lightly and merely ordered to attach himself by a piece of string to the back of the Chairman's Rolls Royce, to be dragged along in its wake, when it sets off for the Chairman's West End club at 1 p.m., after his hard day's work.

Progress In This Year's Cup Ties

However, such extreme measures were not necessary in the case of Ham United this year, because Jock managed to take the club on a reasonable run before being slaughtered to extinction in the Quarter Final. After dispensing with Grimble Town, to cries of "Shame! Shame!", "Big Bullies!", in the Third Round, Ham United went on to meet Northgate Nutters, another of the humble little non-League sides who had escaped extinction in the early rounds. True to the fairy tale nature of the Cup, Northgate are composed of butchers, bakers, candlestick makers and fairies whose life-long ambition in amateur football has been to kick the living daylights out of a First Division football team. Now their great day has come.

However, underdogs visiting big team's grounds are very different from the reverse. To put it at its simplest, after Northgate had battled their way through the crowds of Spivs, Con-men, Groupies, Pickpockets, Bovver Boys, Ticket Touts, and Sociologists doing a survey on the effect of city life on naive yokels just up from the country, they did not have much energy left for doing anything on the field. Which is the way most country cousins go when they have to come to the big city to fight their Cup Ties.

Then, as often happens, the next team Ham United met in this year's competition was Muggingthorpe, a side that they were due to meet again in a League match shortly afterwards.

Such a draw is always well received by Managers, because it makes their job a lot simpler. Meeting the same team in two consecutive matches means they will not have to revise the complex kicking instructions given to the team in the last team talk. The players like such a cup game too because it gives them a chance to settle personal feuds and vendettas that would otherwise have to wait for months to be resolved till the return League match. And of course, any side playing another twice in the space of one week or so is fascinating subject material for Sociologists.

In this case, Ham United's game against Muggingthorpe was quickly resolved in a bloodbath. The reserves of both sides were fielded in the following League match between the two sides while the first team players recovered in hospital, and Ham United scraped through to the next round due to a lucky 89th minute penalty decision and a wad of fivers, the size of a football, changing hands in the referee's dressing room.

Out Of The Cup

The draw for the next round, however, brought bad news to the Londoners. They were drawn away to Brevington Breezers, a team of super-fit 6 ft. 8 in. Yorkshiremen who take not very kindly to being beaten at home and are prepared to stoop to Jose Piranha level to avoid sad humiliation. (See next chapter to see what *that* means.) Northern teams are renowned for liking less of the Good Life, and taking their football relatively seriously, as compared to their Southern brethren. They are even rumoured to abstain from their groupies for two days before every match.

Ham United were 2–0 down at half time, and only a verbal roasting from Jock made them come out for the second half. Some of the effete members of the team had to be retrieved from the showers for the resumption of the game in the second half. I have omitted the final score, as a personal favour to Fingers, who otherwise would tend to want to strangle me with his bare hands.

Is It Fixed?

Such ignominous exits are not at all unusual for the Cup holders. As last year's winners, they are a prime target for every playing maniac in studs. Some people say the Winners of the Cup come from a different part of the country every year because it is all fixed by the old-boys' network of Directors and Chairamen all of whom want a slice of glory, and feel that if one club keeps on winning the Cup every year, too much glory would accrue to one Manager. I am sure such sordid stories have no basis in fact, and they certainly have no place in a dignified handbook about football such as this one.

Where All The Tickets Go

Last year, however, was *the* year for Ham United, which more than made up for subsequent ignominious exits from the Competition, not that it made any difference to the players, who do not know what ignominious means. Because they had reached the Final, all the players were allowed 10 Cup Final tickets each. The players, after distributing the tickets among their loved ones, passed them on to Children's Homes, Orphanages, Hospitals and Youth Clubs, who then promptly sold them at five times face value to ticket touts.

Cup Final tickets bring with them many problems. For Cup Final time is a time when football players find they have friends and relatives they never even dreamt of. Last year, with Ham United in the Final, and thus, with an extra large number of tickets for themselves and their hangers-on, Paddy O'Guinness had a phone call at 5 in the morning from his Great Uncle Seamus in Tipperary, wanting to know how the "young lad is doing, after all these years". And "You'll remember me, son. You saw me when I come over for your christening, when you was three weeks. Would you perhaps be having any spare Cup Final tickets?"

Barclay's fifth cousin removed, rang from the West Indies to say that he was dangerously ill, and the doctors gave him only two weeks to live. And he would like just one sight of England before he went to meet his Maker. And if he could just see the Final at the same time, he was sure this would be all the help he needed.

Jock heard from the suppliers of his specially brewed malt whisky. They told him that if he wanted to keep supplies flowing, he would be well advised to dispatch a couple of tickets. Jock scrambled off a couple of tickets by return of post.

And, as with all teams who reach the Cup Final, all the Ham United players heard from birds they had knocked off over the years who threatened to tell their wives if a Cup Final ticket was not forthcoming.

Wembley Is Their Mecca

All Cup Finals are held at Wembley Stadium. In fact, Wembley Stadium is used for practically nothing else. The reason why the Cup Final is not held at more suitable football grounds is that only Wembley affords sufficient parking space for the Rolls Royces of the Directors and Society People who traditionally attend Cup Finals. Also, Wembley is thought to be sufficiently inaccessible for Bovver Boys.

Also, it is felt that Bovver Boys, nonplussed by the wide open spaces and grandiose architecture of the stadium, will forgo their erroneous ways for just once in the year.

The approach to the Stadium is called Empire Way. Sociologists find this significant. You may or may not. Either way, Empire Way is a wide and extremely long straight road, leading to the very doors of the sacred stadium. The road was so designed in order to impress on ignorant provincial sides the awesomeness and significance of the occasion, and to accommodate all the Ticket Touts and Souvenir Sellers who make Cup Final day what it is—a Spivs' paradise.

This should give the uninformed reader a clue to the true reasons for the existence of Wembley and Cup Finals. More commerce in shabby goods is done on Cup Final Day than is done outside football grounds all over the country in the rest of the season. It provides an unparalleled opportunity for religious cranks to assail the masses. A Cup Final would not be a Cup Final without

batteries of Ticket Touts and Prepare To Meet Thy Doom lads massed along the sides of Empire Way. As in all situations where sharp minded business men gather to exploit their fellow man, a combination of interests comes not amiss—at most Cup Finals these days, you can buy tickets for the End of the World.

Why All Ticket Cup Finals?

The reason for All Ticket Cup Finals is simple. There are so many parasites hovering along the approach to the stadium, that it was felt that any supporter starting off at one end of Empire Way with his entrance money clutched in his hand, would be bankrupt by the time he reached the other end and the turnstiles into the ground. In spite of this, Sociologists foresee a day when there will be so much going on outside the stadium that people will not bother to go in.

At this stage, you may well ask, why go to all this trouble just to give players a bit of novelty in their nasties, and Sociologists food for yet more thought. You might suspect that the whole thing is set up by a horde of Con-Men and Ticket Touts who saw an unparalleled opportunity to line their own pockets under the guise of a great National Sporting Competition. And you might well consider yourself to be quite right.

How To Treat A Tout

Since Ticket Touts are such an essential part of Cup Final Day, as well as being an integral part of the normal football scene, of course, it is important that you be able to recognise these gentlemen of leisured swindle, and to know how to negotiate with them while at the same time retaining the bulk of your ten fingers.

The average Tout is unmistakeable in wide striped suit, red shirt with matching blue tie, pencil thin moustache and slightly tilted panama hat. Further distinguishing points are the Mark 10 Jaguar parked by his side, and the drooling figure of a Sunday Colour Supplement journalist parked by his other side, doing a feature on the colourful characters of the National Game. No Ticket Tout is known ever to have actually watched a game.

The prices he charges vary according to various market forces; namely, how much he thinks he can screw out of you and how much alimony his ex-wives are demanding that week. But, as a rough guide, it can safely be said that a wife and car will always be taken as a fair swop for a £1 standing ticket, and that Mortgage, Colour TV and Three Years' Earnings should bring you a seat in reach of the Royal Box. If, when you get inside, you find that you are nowhere near the Royal Box, you can take it from an experienced hand that your friend outside on Empire Way sends his regrets, and did not know that the Royal Box has been moved since last time.

Not everyone who goes to Wembley has to resort to Ticket Touts for their opportunity. Some people say the Cup Final is a massive social occasion attended by Dignitaries and Hangers-on from most walks of life except football, who buy and sell tickets among themselves as 'perks' for a general social occasion. I am sure such accusations are totally unfounded, and even if there were some truth in them, they have no place in a dignified Handbook about Football like this one.

I can completely refute such scurrilous accusations by quoting the breakdown of the normal attendance at a Wembley Cup Final. Sociologists tell us that every Cup Final Crowd contains 10,000 of their good selves, 20,000 Socialites, 10,000 Titled and Pompous People from various walks of life like hunting, shooting and fishing, 10,000 Bloated Chairmen and Directors, 10,000 Obscure Officials from the obscure Football Associations scattered around the country, 15,000 Con Men and Assorted Spivs, without whom the whole thing would grind to a halt anyway, 5,000 Psychologists, 48 Supporters, 32 Ministers of Sport, the latter being a particularly good wheeze for getting into Cup Finals, because no one knows who is the Minister of Sport. Any football supporter wishing to attend the Cup Final has to write off three months in advance, stating his reasons in writing, enclosing lots of money and a certificate of non-hooliganism, with no guarantee of getting a ticket or his money back.

CHAPTER TEN

England, Europe, The World!!

Win a free place on the tailplane of England's chartered flight to Germany next month!!! Yes, you can fly with the England team, and watch their Game against Germany merely by completing this sentence in not less than 16 words, "We will rout the Krauts because . . . ."

Then detach the special vouchers from the edge of The Football Handbook To End All Football Handbooks, *and send 60 of these along with a sack of money, to: Bent Tours, Mugswelcome, Never-Arrive, The Little Hut at the End of Luton Airport Runway, Disappearquick.*

AFTER the last game of the season, a dreary drawn game against Wearyside Wanderers, a boring Northern team doomed to relegation, Robby and friends suddenly turn up in exotic places like Hong Kong, Honolulu and Japan, teaching the natives a thing or two about football and bagging birds.

This is the Foreign Tour, also known as the Tour Abroad, also known as Going Round the World Just to Play Football with Bunches of Ignorant Foreigners. It is the time when football players, worn out to the point of utter exhaustion, finally finish their punishing programme of fixtures, and recuperate by going abroad and there starting to play with each other and sundry foreigners.

For some lucky players, this will not be the first time in a season that they have been abroad. Clubs that win competitions in this country are invited to go and compete with similarly victorious teams on the Continent. Sensible teams refuse this request, since the Continent is known to harbour some cloggers who would make Mugsy's studs wilt. Also, foreigners are reputed not to eat steak. Clubs also often refuse the thoughtful invitations from nice men with foreign accents, because it is thought the whole experience may be too much for lads who have never been outside a set of English floodlights in their whole life.

Waving The Flag

For those teams that go abroad on tours, it is a matter of making the British Empire flourish again. English teams far and wide stick one on the damn foreigners in a manner not seen since half the Globe was coloured red with British possessions. War Correspondents send in dispatches from Hong Kong and the other aforementioned silly places where football teams go touring, reporting on the state of the battle and enemy casualties.

The first stop on Ham United's Foreign Tour this year was Japan, this being judged the most inaccessible place for the Skull End members who take their aggro world wide. The matches against miniscule Japanese opponents did not go all that well, however. Mugsy spent the first 20 minutes of every game looking in vain for his lumbering opponent to kick and intimidate. Only after some considerable time had passed did anyone summon up the courage to tell him that little 2 ft. 6 in. Japanese men had been nipping round his kneecaps, and knocking in goals like pinballs for the previous 30 minutes.

On arrival in Japan, each member of the team was presented with a kimono for his wife, and a Japanese doll. Mugsy ate his doll, while Vincent said he would wear his kimono at the next home game.

Down Under

The next stop on the tour was Australia. This is always an easy one, and rates top priority on Manager's tour itinerary. Here, our heroes played teams like Wootatong Wanderers and Botany Bay XI, winning by scores such as 16–0. After several matches had resulted in scores like this, Fingers started to fall asleep repeatedly in the match, and had to be brought round with a whiff of Jock Maul's home-made malt whisky. On the journey home, Ham United dropped into the North East Congo for a friendly against a Witch-doctors' XI.

Letters Home

At this point on the tour, Jock told all the players that they must send postcards home to their loved ones, something which is always a severe test of the integrity and intelligence of the players. Before Jock intercepted his postcard, Sid Scythe had written on his postcard: " 'ope you is all rite; I am. The birds 'ere are grate. See you soon", addressed to "My Old Girl, London, Home".

In intricate situations like this, Brains was once again called on to display his unique abilities, and help with the writing of the postcards. This he did in between keeping a tab on the horrendous amounts accruing in debts in the card school, which continued non-stop from Blood Park to Singapore.

Few footballers can bear to be away from home for long. They spend most of their Foreign Tours ensconced in their hotels, snarling at the same reporters they snarl at, week-in-and-out, at the ground, who have been detailed to follow the team abroad and trying to impress ignorant little Oriental chambermaids with the dubious charisma of the English Footballer. To keep in touch with home, Jock sent back urgent cables to his mother in Aberdeen, asking for more supplies of his malt whisky. Davy wrote home to his mother, saying he was homesick, and could she please send him some of those anti-sunstroke pills? When they got to Moscow Robby Score posed in the nude, in the centre spread of *Soviet Women Machinists' Weekly.*

At this point on the tour, the team's supply of steak ran out, so it was time to return home for another year.

Away To Easy Victories

Most teams tend to leave the country very abruptly at the end of the Season. This is because most football clubs tend to have unsuccessful Seasons. There are only half a dozen trophies to go around nearly 100 clubs, even with the very silly made-up competitions that the Pompous People's Committee invents to pacify lousy sides that cannot win the proper competitions. So sides that have won nothing get out of the country as quickly as possible, to avoid furious fans who might otherwise be tempted to lynch the Manager or burn down the Main Stand.

The fans' aggression is in fact the only reason that the Season ends at all. All the teams immediately meet up with each other again when they fly to their tours in Majorca, Africa, Japan or wherever. Here, The Game continues in lighter vein (the clogging being done in plimsolls).

Once safely away from the fans' wrath, the Managers send home reports of their runaway 20–0 victories over Woomera Wanderers and a Spanish Waiters XI, along with other hopeless local sides in Majorca and other favourite tour destinations, to placate the home fans, who even now are burning effigies of the Manager and Chairman in the middle of the pitch back home.

Promises! Promises!

At around this time, it is also customary to issue strongly worded statements on what the team is going to achieve next season, whatever its failings in the Season just past. Even as the First Team squad are staggering exhausted on to the airport tarmac in London, groping for their BOAC jet to freedom, the Manager—or if the Manager has been sacked, as is usually the case, the Chairman—is issuing a stirring blood-and-thunder statement from his oak-lined study on what the team is going to achieve next season. All of which is completely unknown to the players themselves, who are limping exhausted up the stairs to the aeroplane, too exhausted even to give the Stewardess a passing grope on the way in.

Back home at the ground, the Chairman is pounding the table with invective on what his particular team is going to achieve the following season.

The promises are fairly standard; hard tackles will be made, and none shirked. Wingers will score goals, Full Backs will overlap, and the whole team will bounce back in September with renewed vigour and determination. "We fear no one; we underestimate no one; our target is the League/Cup/League Cup/2nd Division Championship/3rd Division Championship/4th Division Championship. Nothing less than that will satisfy us, or our supporters. Our supporters are the greatest. The coming season is going to be one of the greatest in the history of the club." More than 80 Chairmen and a dozen or so twitching Managers are delivering this statement from oak-panelled rooms, at exactly the same time. The dozen or so Managers who are still left with their jobs at the end of the Season (those it may be assumed who have unusually attractive daughters, to retain the Chairman's favour over such a long period as a whole season) are reading their prepared statements sitting at the Chairman's feet.

Meanwhile, the worthy gladiators who are going to achieve all this next September, are collapsing exhausted in the aisles of the First Class cabins of their planes, hanging grimly on to the tailplane, being violently sick in the Loo, and praying that their plane is the one that the Arab guerrillas have decided to hi-jack that week.

The Close Season

While the players leave, the football world takes stock of the season just ended. Reporters who have made incorrect predictions for the season's honours are asked to submit their resignations in writing, and jump from the top floor of their office building with their typewriters around their necks. Reporters whose predictions have come true, are asked to join the players on their three month world-wide booze-and-birds binge. Meanwhile, antique gentlemen are wheeled in from the country to do the summer's reporting on cricket. While, back in the grounds, the last blood is drained off the pitch, the last dead spectators are scraped off the terraces, and the piles of mouldy sandwiches in the club's snackbar which the club has again failed to impress on patrons are stored away for the following season. Since football will not be in the public eye for three months, and thus temporarily not worth its weight in prestige, the Chairman will move his Rolls Royce from its prominent position in the club's car park to a prominent position at The Oval Cricket Ground.

The Close Season, the name for this period of the year when football is not played, is not entirely devoid of football activity. Managers find it a useful time to steal away from the scrutiny of their players and buy fresh stock—new players, that is. While elderly crowd favourites whom the Manager would never dare cast out in the full glare of the season, are quietly escorted to the Knacker's Yard.

It is the time, though, when football inevitably loses some of its news value. The football reporters, or at least those who have not blotted their copybooks in the foregoing season, follow the teams out to Morocco, South Africa and the South Seas, not of course to enjoy a slice of the Good Life, like the players, but to report on the development of The Game in uncivilised parts.

For the footballers themselves, it is a working holiday with the normal routine of training, playing football, getting drunk, wife-swapping and groupie groping. The football reporters, on the other hand, are merely required to sit stoned in the midday sun, drowsily watching their subjects sweat themselves to extinction in the tropical conditions, looking up every now and again to note the new tactical formations that will be spawned in the English First Division in the following season, which is the reporters' justification for coming along on the ride.

However, football reporting has to be severely curtailed in the Close Season, because a large number of teams have their tours in remote parts of Africa, and it is customary for the local Witch-doctors to cut the telephone wires when they see football teams settling in for a stay. They feel their people have caught enough of the White Man's diseases already.

Sacking Of Managers

With the glare of publicity off The Game for a while, now is a very good time to sack Managers, not that the average Chairman needs much encouragement at the leanest of times. However, the discerning Chairman is aware that if you sack a Manager in mid-season, with hundreds of press men crawling around the ground, groveling for a story, it makes your Manager appear a martyr and a scapegoat for the failings of others.

But the wise Chairman waits until after the season, when he can shoot a Manager with relatively little notice being taken of his action. Normal procedure is for the Manager to be shot and/or decapitated in the First Team gym, while the ground is empty after the end of the season, and for his body then to be thrown in the car park.

Most clubs prefer to use more subtle methods, however, although removing a Manager is a routine event in the everyday life of a football club. Foreign tours provide an unequalled opportunity for merciful sacrifice. Many Managers are given a one-way ticket for the team's first destination on the tour. It is regarded as an occupational hazard in the business to find yourself stranded in the remoter parts of Africa, Asia or New Guinea, left with nothing to do but teach football to the natives. (Who, in the case of Head-hunters and Cannibal Tribes, already know a thing or two about football, thank you, very much.) A Manager left stranded, on Chairman's instructions, in the wilds of New Guinea after an unsuccessful season, with a tribe of head hunters and shrinkers, can be said to be keeping in touch with the roots of The Game. Many a pansy Manager has been able to re-order his priorities, and rediscover the true spirit of The Game after being dumped in the wilder parts of Asia or Africa.

Where To Go In The Summer

Some hooligans follow their teams on tour; and take their trail of mayhem across several continents. Attila the Hun was in fact a football fan, who was merely following his team as they went on tour in Italy.

The team's sudden disappearance to the far corners of the Globe presents problems for the average hooligan, who has not yet perfected his technique of hi-jacking. Some hooligans try to compensate for this by vainly trying to initiate their Bovver into cricket and other sundry boring summer sports. However, this has never really caught on. At Lords Cricket Ground last summer two cricket teams played on, oblivious of four ranting Skinheads who were standing outside the Tavern Bar, throwing toilet rolls on to the pitch, screaming abuse at players who were far out of earshot, kicking over empty

spectator benches, ripping out wooden fences with their bare teeth, and brandishing their sharpened steel combs at the remainder of the crowd, two elderly gentlemen, who remained slumped asleep in their seats for the duration of the performance. After half an hour, they gave up, and left. They moved on to an Athletics Meeting, and tried in vain to stir up bovver there, but were perplexed by the running around in circles, and fled at the sound of the starter's gun. To their intense indignation, they thought they had found a sport that attacked its spectators, instead of the other way around.

The Pitfalls Of Winning

Clubs that actually win something are usually at something of a loss about what to do at this stage of the season. They normally spend a day or two parading their Trophy, be it The Cup or League Championship, before their faithful loyal fans, who have supported them through thick or thin, usually through thickness, and who, this time last year, were calling for the Manager's blood. After endless receptions in the Town Hall, where players mingle with civic dignitaries—meeting Magistrates they have not seen since they were put on probation in their wild youth, the players run off on a non-stop booze-and-birds binge until the beginning of the new season.

Thus all the Manager's efforts are employed in trying to recall the bulk of his First Team squad for the start of the new season. From this, it can be seen why clubs that win something one season, rarely manage to retain it for the following season. The Cup, in particular, is a very difficult honour to retain in the following season. Players spend the two months after the Cup Final talking through their winning goals on the television, before dashing off to the binge that lasts into the new season and the return of ordinary League football.

Into Europe

However, once in European competition, the average football club is too geared into the multifarious goodies that can be obtained in that arena, to worry about such a mundane matter as playing for keeps in domestic competitions. Prominent among the goodies are the exceedingly large piles of money to be accrued from the hordes of fans who turn up to gaze at foreign opposition, and to count the number of heads that Russian opponents have.

Most terrace folk are severely disappointed to discover that foreign footballers are of the same variety of two legged, two armed, one headed, sadists as our own lads out there. Nevertheless, matches such as Ham United v Bulgarian Bopzzwechtz, are nearly always calculated to bring thousands of teeth-gnashing, brawling, mauling, blood-hungry average supporters through the turnstiles, hoping to see 11 fire-breathing Gorgons.

The anti-climax at the sight of 11 neo-human beings is compensated for by the rightful wrath which crowds are able to work up at the foreigners' *tactics*.

European football is even more boring and defensive than English football, capable of being played by a spaghetti-eating Chipmunk of the lowest intellect. Such greasy, disreputable football is played at a snail's pace by the foreigners, who, in their shifty, untrustworthy way, knock the ball about amongst themselves, and spend whole periods of the game in their own half of the field. Such disgusting carryings-on are calculated to incense any true-blooded Englishman, and incite him to crash studs into the side of the first sleazy, creepy foreigner he can reach.

Eyeball To Eyeball

While in turn, such fierce tackles are hotly disliked by the aliens, who feel it is one thing to be a pig with the ball, to spit at opponents, pull their hair and pull the little hairs in their kneecaps while they go to kick the ball, BUT it is quite another matter to engage in such physical contact when attempting to *obtain* the ball. What cowards! What unmanly men! You may well wish to join me in saying! Still, as you might gather from this, European games are blood baths, and in the context of run-of-the-mill League game blood-baths may be considered to be The Bloodbaths to End All Bloodbaths.

The situation is further complicated by the fact that teams on the Continent play to different rules from English teams. To suit their own dubious purposes, and since they could not abide by the fair and square rules of Englishmen, the Continentals invented their own rules. This in turn necessitated a neutral referee who would referee without a slavish adhesion to either set of rules. Hence, the demand for short-sighted, incoherent Albanians, who will keep out of the way and let the lads settle things in their own way.

The club's programme for European matches invariably says pompous things about a "clash of cultures". Which indeed it is. Spitting, hair-pulling, eye-gouging and bum-pinching from the foreigners, and good old-fashioned bone-crunching, limb-tearing, stud-crashing stuff from our own lads. It is exceedingly rare to have a European Cup Tie that does not lead to at least one Diplomatic Incident between the countries of the teams concerned. More than one observant person (there are believed to be two of them in football) have said that the European Cup is worth its weight in gunboats.

Trouble-Free Early Rounds

The early stages of European competitions are relatively blood free, however. This is because the teams are seeded, and the big teams are drawn against exceedingly silly little teams from Iceland,

Andorra and Ruritania. These are dispensed with to the tune of 20–0, before the real stuff starts. In the first round of the European Cup last year, Ham United were drawn against Cork Whimsicals, Ireland's most successful team, or at least, so they had told the Entrance Examining Board for the European Cup. The First Leg of the game in Ireland was watched by six local farmers, four priests, 15 cows, 27 hens, four goats, six horses, and 58 bored sheep. It was played in Paddy O'Malley's back garden, and Mrs. O'Malley provided cups of steaming hot cocoa at half time. The score reached 33–0 for Ham United, before the silly little Norwegian referee who was running the game lost count.

Ham United's other matches in Europe last year were against Gringo Athletic, Sorrento Sleazies, Kraut Dynamoes, Dago Rovers and the Consolidated United Steelworkers Machinists and Foundry Workers, Women's Section Number 1179, the Ukraine.

Loyal Fans

There are a loyal group of fans who follow the team even when they go abroad, and who think nothing of chartering a plane out to a remote mountain village in Italy for a couple of days. There is no sight so splendid as thousands of the 'Fish and Chip Brigade', as these folks are called, descending on a simple Italian village, whose team Ham United are due to play, and fighting like maniacs over the single three-week-old copy of the *Daily Mirror* which arrives by donkey every day from Naples. The steel comb lads among the expeditionary force go spaghetti bashing for the duration of their stay.

The Con-Men and Spivs who surround every League club, also make the journey out to foreign parts and often, for the first time, meet their match in their Continental counterparts. An Italian Con-Man trying to sell the Leaning Tower of Pisa to an English Con-Man who is trying to sell him the Houses of Parliament for the second time, is regarded as Con-Man's Deadlock. Such horrendous deadlocks are usually resolved by both parties combining to fleece the hell out of their compatriots who are searching for match tickets.

Choose Your Tour

However, if you are not a Bovver Boy or a Con-Man, and are that rarity amongst football folk, a *supporter*, your prospects are not so simple. In their never ending efforts to bring the masses to football, football to the masses, and masses of money to themselves, Bent Tours Ltd., who were last seen leaving by the back door of the Little Hut on the end of Luton Airport runway, constantly organise a series of all-in package holidays for addicts who have to go abroad to keep getting their fix. Bent Tours run four separate schemes for travelling supporters, and they are as follows:

(1) Rich Man's Tour, £200. Pick the team, and include yourself. Give your own team talk, lunch with the Directors, and have your picture taken with Vincent.

(2) Almost as Rich Tour, £150. Choose the team, design their shirts, and have a meal with them. Stay in the local Hilton, and have your picture taken with Brains.

(3) Average Tour, £90. By coach to the match, in time to see the team arriving at the ground. Have your picture taken with Mugsy. Watch your hotel being built. Hamburger vouchers to the value of 40p provided.

(4) Bovver Tour, £40. Journey in the cattle truck of your choice. Those of the party not in the 'nick' after 24 hours, are invited to share the apes' cages in the local zoo.

There is one other route for getting abroad in the name of football, and that is the esteemed honour of being picked to play for your country. The criterion for getting selected for England (apart from not knowing what big words like "criterion" mean) is to be the biggest kicker of players, in your particular position, in the country.

How To Get Into The England Team

It is therefore very helpful if your side are due to play the teams containing your rivals for an England shirt shortly before selection for the final England Team takes place. Selective maiming has on many occasions led to an England place for an otherwise hopeless candidate. This is what is called, "determination making up for lack of skill", a well known and used football phrase that hides a multitude of super Nasties.

However, this has sometimes been taken too far, and there have been instances of the poorest Inside Right in the country setting out to cripple the other 21 in the course of First Division football, in order to inherit the England number eight shirt over the bodies of his erstwhile competitors. So that the supply of possible Cloggers to the England side would not dry up, the Disciplinary Rules of Football were invented, whereby any player found committing a given number of Horrors in a given space of time on one player who was a potential England candidate, would be fined 5p and told not to do it again.

South American Cloggers

However, the Cloggers of England and of Europe pale in comparison with the Cloggers of South America. This may not be unrelated to the fact that a large number of Nazi war criminals fled to South America after the Second World War, and are known for the most part to have become Football Coaches and Managers. South American pitches are surrounded by moats, patrolled by crocodiles, into which the foolish wounded from pitch and terrace are thrown.

Last year, Ham United were mugs enough to accept an invitation to a 'friendly' match in Buenos Aires against a South American Nasties XI, a combined side of the five most horrific South American sides. The South Americans had caught wind of Ham United's heinous reputation, and wanted to see if they had anything to learn from the Gringos. Suffice to say, for match report, that there was not much.

The match was conducted under the capable supervision of Senhor Foula Blinda, from Bormann, Argentina. The weakest of the Argentinians made Mugsy look like a Maiden Aunt. The wounded from the match were thrown in the River Plate, for the piranhas.

Piranhas, you may not know, are named after a particularly vicious Uraguayan Full Back of the last century, Jose Piranha, who was reputed to be able to strip a man's leg to the bone on the first tackle. He was made a National Hero, with Jose Piranha Day being held every year on the anniversary of his 1,000th victim. Towns and villages were named after him; he was remembered in the country's revised National Anthem : 'The Ballad of Jose Piranha'; schoolchildren were exhorted to "tackle in the manner that Brother Jose would have approved of"; the Piranhaist Political party came to dominate the political life of the country; and the previously named Football Fish was re-named in his honour. Never has one Full Back made such a lasting impression on the social and cultural life of one country.

CHAPTER ELEVEN
A To Z Of Football And Things

If you had read this chapter in the first place, you would not have needed to have read the rest of the book.

Attacker
1. A player who plays in the attack of the team, which is why he is called an Attacker. Also known as a Forward, because he plays forward of the team, in his efforts to get goals.
2. Someone who attacks the Referee because he thinks he is a fat, short-sighted, narrow-minded little pig who should have that player off for kicking that other player like that.

Ball
Small, round object that has to be kicked into the net of the other team, for any team to have scored a goal. In ancient days, human heads were used, and there are still those in the game today who would like to see a return to this tradition.

Ball Winner
Polite term for member of the team whose job it is to obtain the ball from the other side by any means possible. Has not got the faintest idea what to do with the ball once he has it, so is often accompanied by a *skilled player*.

Boot
1. Item of equipment worn by footballers for kicking ball.
2. Item of equipment worn by *Bovver Boys* for kicking people. Both tend to be covered in blood before the season is very old.

Bovver
The result of *Bovver Boys*.

Bovver Boys

1. Modern youth, disaffected by the underlying materialistic precepts of this society.

2. A group of lads whose main interest is in kicking the hell out of each other.

Chairman

The top man at any Football Club. Tends to be rich, pompous, egotistical, patronising, and knows nothing about football. Usually owns the club in some subtle way or another, or is milking the hell out of it, or using it as a springboard for his business interests. Most Chairman like to treat 'their' Football Club as an exhibit to be shown off to potential business clients. No Chairman has ever been known to hold a conversation with a footballer for more than 30 seconds.

Coach

Man who tells the players what to do in their training. Afterwards, they tell him what to do.

Committee Of Pompous People In Charge Of Football

The bosses of football. Football is like most things in that however much it is about people enjoying themselves, ultimately it is governed by a group of bald, ageing windbags, who, in this particular case, would not know a footballer, let alone a football, if they saw one.

The Committee, who, in this modern democratic day and age, are unelected, are selected from the Boards of the various better known Football League clubs. One member is selected from the less successful clubs, because he is exceptionally old and has lots of money, and to keep the Lower Divisions happy.

These are the men who have to make all the important decisions about The Game. This makes things difficult, because they are the sort of men who do not like changing things—anything at all. The Committee has been in existence for 2,000 years now, and has been known to wake up four times to make a decision.

Con-Men

The nice man in a pinstripe suit who sold you Wembley Stadium last week. Football is full of them. They make their way towards football because there they sense lots of loose money, many naive young footballers and an aged Management that could not pass a law to outlaw Con-Men, even if it were awake. While Managers are only concerned with keeping their jobs, and screaming abuse at their players, day and night. Which leaves lots of room for Uncle Fred, Uncle Harry, Honest Sid, Lenny the Fixer, etc. etc.

Cup

The other main competition, along with the League. In this competition, all the football teams in the country, from your silly local park team that has not won a game for four years, to the First Division's Ham Uniteds, are thrown together in knock-out competition. Often the little teams beat the very big teams that are much better than them. Which shows you what a silly competition it is. Still, psychologists say it is of value because it gives players variety in their opponents. The final of the Cup is played at Wembley, where you can see more touts and con-men on one day than in a whole season of League matches; another of the ways in which the Cup differs from the League.

Defenders

Footballers whose job it is to stop the Opposition scoring. They tend to have less skill than forwards, in fact one might say that they are big, thick, stupid, brutes with the intelligence of a chipmunk. One is advised not to say such things near them; these are the people that do most of the nasties for which football has become famous.

Directors

Football, like everything else, has a Board of Directors. Every Football Club has a Board of Directors. And like Directors every-where, they are ignorant, idle slobs who are just in it for the prestige. They can be distinguished by the lengthy cigar, Rolls Royce, blonde personal assistant sitting on the lap during the game and general all-round repulsiveness.

England

The National team, and the pinnacle to which every footballer aspires. England are the best football team in the world. They do not always win their matches, but that is beside the point. You see more blood in an England match than in at least three League matches. If England do lose, it is because of the referee (being an International match, the referee has to be a foreigner. That is the only reason that England ever lose matches).

European Cup

Teams that do well in the League compete in this, with all the other successful teams from Europe. Some people refer to it as the 'Cloggers' Festival', since you get all the different teams clogging each other in distinct ways, but I am sure this is unfair. Some people also say that Britain had to join the Common Market in order to be in a position to arbitrate the multiple Diplomatic Incidents that arose from the European Cup. I am sure this is not true.

Footballers

People who play football, go to night clubs at four in the morn-ing, screw each others' wives, say silly things in the papers, judge beauty competitions, open shops, appear in plastic form in every other cereal packet in the country and also appear as themselves on telly every Saturday night.

Foreigners

People who also play football, but not so well, and they do nasty things like spit at you and gouge you in the eye. Also, they are better able to bribe referees because they have more worthless currencies than our British Pound. A walloping great roll of Italian banknotes on a referee's floor looks better than the pile of good old British fivers that is rolling around there too, although the Italian wad is only worth 5p.

Foul

The technical name for a Nasty committed by one player on another player. There are several recognised forms of fouls; the elbow in the stomach as a tackle is made; the harsh tackle, where the man's foot gets clobbered before and harder than does the ball; the head-butt; the kick in the back; the bite of the leg; the chicken wire around the neck; the tickle of the Oooglies are all well known and loved fouls that can be found on any English football field in any match.

Hard Tackle

Cover name for a particular Foul (see above). A player goes for a tackle at 100 miles an hour instead of 20, and the poor man, who had the ball, loses both legs in an amputation, and goes spinning across the pitch like yesterday's reserve team ball. The referee goes up to the tackler and tells him not to do it again, because he saw that. If he does it again he will take the tackler's name.

Intellectual Supporters

Recent addition to the terraces. Not many of them around, but half a dozen of them sprinkled around a crowd of 50,000 is sufficient to raise the combined IQ of assembly by 500 per cent. They are very much out of place in any football crowd, dressed in their shabby duffle coats, intense glasses and polo neck sweaters; but as such, they are the only things ever known to stop a Bovver Boy in his tracks. Ironically, they tend to congregate around the less-skilled clubs, and find deep meanings in the crudest of tackles.

Intelligence

Misprint: has got nothing to do with the subject or content of this book. I don't know how it got here.

Kicking

Several meanings: (1) V.tr. Kicking the ball (rare).

(2) Kicking the player on opposing side, to give advantage to your own side.

(3) V.tr. An action committed by a Bovver Boy.

Kicking (3) is illegal, and defendants are heavily fined, sentenced to Detention Centres, etc. Kicking (2) is slightly illegal if you do it a lot and a lot and a lot of times, and you have been caught each time (rare).

League

The basis of football competition in this country. All the professional teams are organised into a League of teams that play each other twice throughout the season, before ending up with the final league table that decides who goes into Europe and who goes into the never-never regions below. The 3rd and 4th Divisions are regarded as a sort of football fiery pit, from which there is seldom redemption. While Europe is Heaven.

League Cup

Just to complicate matters, there has to be this, called both League and Cup. Simply, it's another Cup, but not as important as THE CUP (which is much bigger, anyway). It is a Cup competition open only to teams that are in the League, in other words, the better class of team. A sort of snobs' Cup, but not as exciting, because without the silly little teams, you don't have the romance, and the chance of a really big upset.

Linesman

Silly little man who runs along the side of the pitch, while the game is in progress, waving a coloured flag every now and again. No one takes any notice of him until there is a disputed point, which invariably means Offside, and the referee consults him then. Linesmen can also have a lot to do with disallowing goals, but this is a rare duty, because goals are rarely scored these days. Most of them are failed Semaphore Men.

Manager

Neurotic person who runs a football team. To some extent, it is a duff job in that footballers being so thick, there is absolutely nothing you can teach them. So Managers are employed on their shouting basis—their ability to shriek, shout, bully and abuse their players into action. For this reason, many clubs prefer to employ Scots, whose accent makes it impossible to tell what they are saying, and makes it thus sound all the more threatening. Very few Managers stay in the same job for more than a fortnight, the casualty rate being high to the point of putting the Battle of the Somme to shame. Most Managers end up throwing themselves under their Chairman's Rolls Royce, as stipulated in the suicide clause of their contract.

Midfield

Not surprisingly, the middle of the field. It is widely thought in football, in so far as anything is widely thought in football, that if a team controls the middle of the pitch—that is, if it puts the boot about there so much that the Opposition is white-hot scared to venture there—then they have the game all but won. So midfield is where most of the action takes place.

Mugs

You, for buying this book. Foreign teams that accept invitations to play English teams in 'Friendly' matches; anyone who accepts an invitation to play a South American team in a 'Friendly' match.

Offside Rule

The most misunderstood rule in football, where scarcely anyone takes any notice of the rules, anyway. But everyone pretends to understand the Offside Rule. In fact, it is quite simple; a player may not score a goal unless there are at least two members of the Opposition between him and the goal at the time. One of these must be the goalkeeper. However, if the Moon is in the Ascendant, and the goalkeeper's birthday is in Capricorn, the obverse is true, and the goal will only be allowed to stand if the preceding pass was from an opponent with green hair who ate steak for dinner before he came out. Understand?

Pools

The Pools were invented by a failed Noughts and Crosses player. You are given a silly but very complicated coupon, with all the fixtures for that week down one side, and a huge sea of squares down the other side of the page. The idea is that you put a cross against every fixture that you think will be a draw, and if you get them all right, you win lots of money. The pools are generally won by little old ladies who stick in their hat pins at random, or infuriating people from Cleethorpes, who have their photos taken wearing masks, saying they want no publicity, but you can still see that they are grinning inanely.

The other type of pools winner is that of the Syndicate. Here 38 people, usually from Scunthorpe, have banded together in a consortium. They make the journey down to the big city to collect their £356,000, and do a knees-up and drink champagne for the press. They eat out at the poshest restaurants, and then have to return 2nd class to Scunthorpe after a couple of days because they have spent all the money, or given it to the nice man who said he would sell them the Houses of Parliament in return for Scunthorpe Town Hall, but would be willing to take cash in the meantime.

The Press

People who write about football. The press was invented as an aid to football fans unable to get to matches because of their injuries from last week's hooliganism. Television, in a similar way, was invented, as a stop gap for those supporters who could not wait until Sunday morning to get their fix of the previous day's results. Live radio commentaries, in fact, radio itself, were invented for people who were too stupid to find the ground to go and watch the game themselves. Also, for aged grandmothers, who are football fanatics, and the famed elderly sick relatives of arrested hooligans who want to keep in touch with their son's progress. (See also, *Writing Styles.*)

5—FH • •

Referees

Two major types :

1. Weak referees (common). These are short, fat, insignificant men who have become referees as a long but easy way round to collecting autographs off players, whom they were too frightened to ask when they were just ordinary spectators. Such referees stay a considerable distance from the ball, so while they may hear players uttering rude words to one another—which they will book them for—they will not see the diabolical fouls players do to each other—which they will not book them for.

2. Firm referees (rare). These are discipline maniacs, who took a wrong turning when on the way to a Leather and Discipline party, and ended up at a Referees' Training Course, instead. This is the sort of referee who will not send someone off for breaking another player's leg, but will send off four men for complaining at his not sending off that culprit.

Skilled Player

Dying breed of footballer, who can play good football, and thus does not need to resort to Nasties. Believed to be three in existence.

Skinhead

1. Race of Super Nasties, friends of the Huns and Goths. They invaded Europe, along with them, nearly 2,000 years ago. The Skinheads came West in Football Specials, ripping out seats and smashing the windows as they came. Overwhelmed all of England, except for a small bit just outside Streatham, which they left alone. They came by and by, to settle on football matches in particular, because this was the best place for getting their fix of blood and violence. They can be identified by their short cropped hair, braces holding up their trousers, heavy walking/kicking boots with blood on the end and steel combs. Also, you can tell a Skinhead because they always speak in a basic grunt vocabulary, and never do nice things, even to old ladies. They say they like football. So they smash it up all the time.

2. Disaffected youths, who have found the precepts of modern civilisation to be wanting in all respects.

Stars

Every Club has one or two. Every footballer thinks he is one. But you can tell which one is really the star, because he is the one with no mud on his kit after half an hour and all his team mates are shouting at him. He declines to get involved in the rough stuff, and occasionally tries to turn on whatever skill he may have. He's the face on the posters that are sold to silly little boys outside the ground before the game, and whom they all mob at the end of the game.

Superstar

The most skilful, arrogant, controversial, overpaid, best-looking, most scandalous, member of the team. Superstars are stars who are stars even in a team of stars. The Superstar is the one whose car gets more initials scratched on it than that of any other member of the team. It is taken for granted that in the course of a season a Superstar will have three nervous breakdowns, $4\frac{1}{2}$ runaways, 26 affairs with Bunny Girls, and be seen 17 times in night clubs at four in the morning before a game. They earn more money than the rest of the team put together, and will generally play 15 games out of the 42, scoring 11 hat-tricks, and pulling in thousands of swooning little girls at every appearance.

Substitute
A player who may be brought on to the pitch, in place of another player, at any time in the match. He may be a young player on the verge of the team, an aged veteran, gently being pushed out of the place, or a player with bad breath whom no one can stand having on the pitch for more than five minutes. Substitutes are normally put on when one of the regular team is injured, and has to be withdrawn from the pitch. It is not unknown for the substitute to sneak on to the pitch while the Manager is not looking, and deal a deadly nasty to one of his own side, in order to get a game for himself.

Supporters
Ordinary people who go to watch football, and enjoy it as an entertainment. A declining species; often to be found in the form of father and son. They are believed to have no ulterior motive or vested interest in going to watch games, and are therefore the subject of much sociological study. Thought to be 38 such people left in this country. Disliked very much by the football authorities, who insist that these aggravating people state their reasons in writing three weeks before ever going to see a game.

Tackle
The act of taking the ball from a member of the opposition team. For further information, see *Foul*.

Trainer
Little man in a tracksuit who sprints on with a kit bag, whenever one of his team goes down injured, or just wants a word of reassurance from a Father Figure. Does absolutely nothing else all week; just sprints on with the magic bag, when one of the side gets hurt. When he gets to the player, much wincing takes place (on the part of the player), and much rubbing of thighs, supporting of shoulders, and askings of "Are you all right, lad?" (by the Trainer), take place. The thigh rubbing aspect has been responsible for the attraction of many poofdas into football. Those of that number who have actually reached the trainer's bench, have frequently had to be restrained from some elaborate thigh massaging (when it was the player's shoulder that was hurt in the first place).

Transfer

The act of dispatching one player from a club to another club, which is done because : (1) You, the Manager, do not fancy his wife any more. (2) You, the Manager, do not fancy him any more. (3) He's no bloody good. (4) You felt like selling someone, to boost your ego. (5) The Club is in debt, and the Chairman refuses to cut down on his free brandies at the club's expense, so the only way you can raise money is by selling a player.

TV Commentators

One of the silliest breeds of people in the game. They think it is their job to talk while we are watching football matches on the tele, and tell us what is happening. Some people say football was invented to give these peculiar people a living, because, assuredly, they could not earn a living doing any other job. I am sure such wicked accusations are completely unfounded.

There is no clear route to becoming a Football Commentator, although a lack of wit, honesty and originality are an advantage. A droning voice, and an ability to remember the score and the names of the two sides, are an added asset.

Some commentators are ex-players, who, when swearing at the referee for booking them, found that more than three words came out, and thus discovered their true vocation. But more often, they tend to be bored university chappies, who grew fed up with their surveys of why ordinary people like football so much, and so asked for jobs as commentators, and being so obviously talented, were snapped up.

Wembley Stadium

As the Vatican is to the Roman Catholic faith, so is Wembley Stadium to Football. All Cup Finals are held there. As such, it is regarded as too good for the ordinary football supporter, and few, if any, of these are allowed to pass through the hallowed gates. It is said that the road to Wembley is paved with ticket touts. I am sure that this is untrue, and even if it were true, such an accusation against the spirit of such a hallowed place has no part in a dignified Handbook about Football like this one.

Whizz Kid Managers

The type of Manager who has super go-ahead ideas like teaching his players to think for themselves, telling them to attack whenever they have the chance, and to play by the rules. Such men have generally come into the game by mistake, and most of them get out of it pretty quickly when they see what it is all about. They are not very significant really, and I only included them to prove that not all Managers are cowardly, small-minded, time-servers, frightened to introduce a single bold or original idea into the game.

Writing Styles Of Football Reporters
HAC:
The predominant style of football reporting. Short, sharp phrases and flamboyant clichés are the characteristics of this style, i.e.: "The lion-hearted fighters of Ham United set the football world alight last night with a storming display of attacking football, that stunned Muggingthorpe, and sent them back home from the big city with a stinging reminder of Cockney pride." This style is particularly applicable to International matches, where, for example, the Poles, if it is a Polish team playing, can be "axed". Expression "hac" comes from the action of hacking simple characteristics out of stone, which is how the first Stone Age hacs set about their business.

COLOUR SUPPLEMENT PROSE:
"The day of the football match begins in small ways; football is always about small people, ordinary people, the seemingly insignificant people of life, those that we would not give a moment's glance to, on the tube train, or on the 2nd Floor of Harrods.
"On this Saturday, as on every Saturday morning, one can trace from the faint murmurings, from an early hour, the great roaring tide that will later build up into the crescendo that is the game itself. But at the moment, it is early morning still, and the rosette sellers are ploddingly assembling their positions in . . ." etc., etc.

LONG WINDED MATCH REPORT FOR SUNDAY PAPER:
"One approaches the city over the long, lumbering folds of the Lincolnshire countryside. The fields are starting to come ablaze again with drifting ranks of corn; the waters from the spring rain have faded away now, leaving the ground to mature into the heavy, turbulent mud that is so alien to the Southerners' style of play. One wonders how the temperaments of the Season will affect the incisive wing play of Spooner, that young man so full of promise, yet so prone to erroneous ways . . ." etc., etc.

CHAPTER TWELVE

Substitute Chapter

IF at any time, you find any of the chapters in this Handbook unutterably boring or quite utterly uninformative, you may rip the offending chapter out of its place in the book, and replace it with this chapter, the all-purpose Substitute Chapter, ready and willing to be rushed into action anywhere in an ailing book, at a moment's notice. All football books have been written in this way since football introduced Substitutes, one of the few reform measures that managed to slip through while the Committee of Pompous People in Charge of Football were looking the other way or, as some might allege, sleeping.

Briefly, the Substitute Rule allows a Manager to take any one of his players off the pitch during the game, and replace him with his reserve player, who has been kept in an iron cage, fed the odd limb or two, while his bloodthirsty eyes watch the real action out on the pitch. Substitutes bound on to the pitch with barely concealed pent-up fury at being held back from the action for so long, having to watch others do Nasties that they know they are fully capable of doing given half the chance.

Such a chapter is this. Here we rip aside the myths surrounding the transfer market, to give you the truth of a little-known side of soccer, until now the private domain of a handful of desperate little men who will stoop to anything to preserve their stranglehold on the way free men live their lives. (I am indebted to Fred Fiddlexpenses of The Twitch-on-Sea's *Clarion*, for the preceding line, who gave me my first break in journalism, and whom I promised such a reward when I had made it. Do you know how many men there are in a football team, yet, Fred?)

The decision to sign new players is one of the more misunderstood sides of football. Players are signed because the club has an ageing rustic in a particular position, who they know will not last out the season. Or because they need reserve strength. Some people, though, say that players are sometimes signed because the Manager fancies their wife, or because the Chairman is one short in his collection of Top Footballers' Medals from the Petrol station, and can't find the missing one anywhere, so he tells the Manager to go out and buy that player. I am sure such things are not true, and even if they were they have no place in a dignified Handbook about Football, like this one.

Transfers

The transfer market is one of the more misunderstood aspects of football. In the first place, the term is really an understatement of the process. It might be more correctly termed the Buying, Begging, Borrowing, Stealing, Loaning and Kidnapping market. It is the place where any would-be Godfather can learn how to make offers that people simply cannot refuse. The basic idea of the transfer market is quite simple. You, or someone in your club, spot another player at another club who is one hell of a lot better than the player you have in that position in your own Club. What you have to do now, is get him from his club to yours, a game not unlike Monopoly and other games for power-hungry little egomaniacs, the derogatory term that some people apply to Chairmen who force their Managers to splurge huge sums of money on big-name players who could not kick a football if they knew what one looked like.

Scouts

Clubs maintain a network of scouts, whose job it is to watch clubs in their areas, and report on any outstanding prospects. Details are sent out from Blood Park of the type of players required in the immediate future. At any one time, Jock may be looking for a player who can maim quicker than Masher, or scythe 'em down neater than Sid, or one who is better looking than Vincent (better looks = lots of starry eyed little girls coming along to watch their hero = bigger crowds = more £££ = bigger No-Lose bonus for the players = more goals = success = more Prestige for Chairman Knowlesworth-Blair).

Whenever a report is received of a good, likely-looking prospect, a senior scout is dispatched from Blood Park to double check the original scout's report; this is to ensure that the first sighting was not made under the influence of alcohol, or that the scout in question is not trying to sneak his own son, or private prodigy, into League Football.

A Likely Lad

If, however, the player lives up to expectations on a second showing, the next stage is to get him to put in a transfer request to his present club. This will save you having to bid for the bugger on the open market, which will inflate his vanity to the point of demanding a hefty signing-on fee when changing clubs. Also, bidding on the open market forces the price of players up to dizzy heights, when other clubs join in the scramble for his signature.

(The widely reported concept of a player signing for a club is of course a complete misnomer. Not only is the average footballer quite incapable of writing his name even if he knew it, but would never give his name to anyone even if he could. After all, you never know who might be a Referee, booking you for last week's nasty that you thought you had got away with. Players only sign bits of paper pushed in front of them by their agent, who points to the appropriate spot, and says : "Sign here, son". Contracts on joining new clubs, are one such bit of paper, although even these are often signed by the Agent, ever willing to help out in these situations. And it is the Agent who invariably collects the signing-on fee that clubs give to their new players, always promising to pass on the said fee to the player, in due course. . . .)

When the club is interested in another player, the Manager instructs everyone in the team to take every opportunity to tell the sought-after one what a great player he is. In the case of Ham United, Jock always takes care to instruct Mugsy and Masher to go nowhere near him should the two teams meet in a game at the time.

Setting a Snare

One of the standard ways to make your approach to the target man in question is to arrange a 'Friendly' match with his club. Friendly games are one of the curiosities of football. In the first place, they are the least friendly of all the various types of games played. They are called 'Friendly Games' because they are not League or Cup Games, and are arranged with (apparent) random opposition. This means that the players are kicking each other for the sheer hell of it, and not for any sordid financial gain. The other purpose of a 'Friendly Game' is to give opportunities to the hooligans to fight with other hooligans whom they would not normally meet in the course of the season—much the same purpose, you may remember, is served by the Cup. Psychiatrists say it is good for them.

Contrary to general public opinion, 'Friendly Games' are not arranged with any random load of rubbish. First Division teams, for example, commonly arrange 'Friendlies' with up and coming Second Division sides, so they can give them a foretaste of what is to come when they scale the heights into the Promised Land of the First Division, and so on down the League.

Also, of course, a footballer can learn a thing or two from watching his lesser colleagues from up or down the scale. Mugsy spends hours watching his local park side, looking for hints of clogging that his more sophisticated colleagues would not deign to stoop to.

"Friendlies" are often arranged with Scottish sides, who are universally regarded as pretty thick, and always good for a 10-goal splurge to keep the fans happy when things have not been going too well. These can be combined with scouting expeditions because the Scots produce some pretty hair-raising Cloggers of their own. And any starry-eyed Scots Clogger will jump at the chance to come South to 'Clogger's Paradise', to make his name and repeatedly give it to referees.

Our Foreign 'Friends'

Foreign sides are always good for 'Friendlies' too. If your team is not good enough to qualify for Europe, you can always round up a few Italian waiters, call them 'Italy', and pull off a prestige victory in front of your awestruck home fans. While genuinely good foreign sides are always pleased to accept an invitation to come and play a game in England, because they all regard England as the Mother Country of Football. Foreign teams accepting such invitations are commonly regarded as mugs in English footballing circles, particularly in the centre circle, where the more lustful Cloggers hang out, those who could not wait for the opposition to arrive in front of goal, but who moved up field to confront them. This is because lots of foreign teams still play football by the rules, and have not heard that all English teams have long since abandoned such irrelevant absurdities. On the other hand, some foreign teams have developed Super Nasties who quite dwarf the worst that is dreamt up on an English pitch. This can come as quite a shock to an English side who think they have invited over a group of complete mugs from Ruritania, in order to practise some top-secret Clogging techniques preparatory to unleashing these on the English First Division. They then find that their foreign friends

have developed methods of intimidation that would make any Englishman's studs wilt.

One does not want to name any nationalities of course. This would be detrimental to our foreign relationships and to the general good name of football, but if absolutely pushed, I would say that the Italians, the Greeks and the Turks can all teach us a thing or two about Clogging, while the South Americans are in a Clogging class of their own.

Whatever the ability of the opposition, the basic idea is still to invite over a team of innocent Wops or Krauts, or whatever, and give them the kicking of their lives, just to remind them who is master, rules or no rules, and put out a warning just in case the two clubs should ever meet in European competition proper at some future date. "We might have joined the Common Market, but we can still teach these aliens a thing or two about football", is how Jock put it to me. Jock, it may be added, is still fuming about the Act of Union between England and Scotland 400 years ago: "It was a trick to get all our best players down here for free", he snarls at intervals.

How To Impress A Future Signing

When a club is after a player from another club, it is standard policy to arrange a 'Friendly' against the desired player's club. This way, several things can be achieved. For a start, you get a further idea of the man's playing ability, and although you tell your Choppers to lay off—"Don't spoil the goods" is the common expression—you get an idea of how the man stands up to treatment. Also, you tell your players to have a word with him during the course of the match, and tell him how good life is at Ham United, and what he is missing by staying with this "load of old rubbish". If he is still not interested after 80 minutes, the technique then is to kick the hell out of him unmercifully for the remainder of the match, until he is pulled off with his kit dripping in blood. After profuse apologies, you offer to take him off his present club's hands at a small fee, and see if you can nurse the poor lad back to the living. If the 'Friendly' can be arranged at Blood Park, then so much the better. This gives you a chance to impress the lad with some of the aspects of a footballing organisation that every discerning footballer looks for in a top line club—a well stocked bar, numerous Groupies, all within five miles of the nearest Bunny Club. And if he is still not interested, you can always kidnap him, or threaten to throw him to the Skull End. It is not commonly known that The Godfather learnt how to make offers to people that they could not refuse at his local football club.

'Friendly' games, incidentally, fall outside the scope of the Committee of Pompous People in Charge of Football, one of the few things that does. Therefore, clubs are left free to charge anything they like for admission and Programmes. Which is why some clubs play more 'Friendly' games than League games in a season.

Testimonials

A variation on the 'Friendly Game' is the Testimonial Game. This is a game that is staged in honour of a player who has completed 10 or more years with his club. All the proceeds of the game go to the player concerned. Of course, readers of *The Football Handbook To End All Football Handbooks* will by now know that that is not going to be strictly true; most of the money will end up going to . . . Yes. That's right!—his Agent. But clubs can hardly let this become common knowledge. The Robby Score Testimonial, for example, would not look very good if it were advertised as the Uncle Harry Testimonial, would it? However, the player in question is usually fairly senile by the time his Testimonial comes around (another fact which enables the club and his agent to screw the hell out of the old fool, while he thinks everyone is doing him a great favour), and he willingly accepts the limelight while his better half scoops in all the real rewards.

Nevertheless, custom has to be respected, and the ageing maestro is given every opportunity in the match to show off whatever aged talent he still has, and may perhaps even be allowed to score a goal.

Testimonials are a highly useful way of paying off old Croakers who are otherwise quite impossible to chase out of the woodwork. Ancient old Buzzards who have not kicked a ball since the end of the 1933 season, are allowed to go out in a blaze of glory and cash on the strict understanding that this is their lot, and that if they go blabbing to the press, they won't get their cheque. If there is any suggestion of their not co-operating, Mugsy can always be detailed to take care of the misguided little man while the game is on.

Cloak And Dagger Stuff

Such routine measures are not necessary when a club is striving to wangle another player on to its staff. This is much more a matter of cloak-and-dagger diplomacy. The Manager will take every opportunity to extol the sought-after one's virtues in public. He will repeatedly say that he is so surprised that the man has not been picked for the England team a long time ago. (Although it is always advisable to check whether or not he is English, first. Many a budding transfer move has fallen apart at the last moment, when an irate Irishman has woken up to read in the papers that his prospective Manager think he is on the verge of being picked for the England team.)

If your target is really thick, and still has not taken the hint, the next move is to use direct inducements. These are more commonly known as bribes. Sought-after defenders are offered £50 for every limb they break at their new club; midfield ball-winners are promised £100 for every crunching tackle they make, while for-wards are promised £100 for every goal they score, with the usual admonishments not to overdo it.

How To Arrange A Transfer

When the player finally twigs what is happening—and many players take so long to catch on that the prospective buying club loses interest—the next step is for him to have a couple of very bad games for his present club. This leads, inevitably, to a call into the Manager's office and demands for an explanation for a loss of form. This leaves him free to make his next move, to spin a sob story to explain his playing failures. He may say he is unhappy at the club; that he is not finding football any fun any more; and how all his best friends play for So and So club, which just happens to be the one that he knows is interested in him; that his wife is threatening to leave him if he continues playing for his present club, because she is so fed up with the same blokes every season on the wife-swopping rota, and wants to experiment with a different First Team squad. Everything is tried on, in fact, short of actually asking for a transfer. This is because if a player asks for a transfer, which is thought not to be a nice thing to do, he loses his percentage of the transfer fee.

If the Manager is a softie—a dying breed in the game these days —he will now say: "Yes, that's all right, son, I quite understand. I think you would be much happier if you had a change of club. If there is any club where you feel you would be particularly happy, just let me know, and I will see what I can do."

But if the Manager is one of the tough, no-nonsense, new breed of Managers who have been coming into the game in recent years, a player can expect all hell to be let loose when he tells his sob stories. The standard reaction of the tough, no-nonsense, new breed of Manager who has been coming into the game recently, is to throw a player out of the office, slap a £200 fine on him, double the amount of extra training he is due to do that week, remind him of all the Super Horribles the club can commit, outlined in the small print of his Contract, which the club told him not to bother about reading when he signed it at the time of joining the club, and send him off to clean the Reserve Team's boots for the afternoon.

Several options are open to a player in such a position. Firstly, he can commit suicide. Secondly, he can give in, and grovel at his Manager's feet, say he is sorry, and that he will never, never again ask for a transfer. Or he can tip-off a friendly press man that he is unsettled at his present club, and hope that this will lead to press speculation about his future that will put his Manager under pressure and entice would-be buyers. But this method often fails. The press themselves spend all week floating hundreds of phony "I want out!" stories, and are usually too busy speculating on conceivable grandiose transfer moves to take any notice of a player who says he wants a transfer. It is not worth the player continuing to play his worst on the pitch, because his fines from the Manager will keep piling up, and this diminishes his value to interested clubs, anyway. He can always appeal to the various Committees of Pompous People in Charge of Appeals and Arbitration and Important Sounding Things, but by the time they have all been woken up, and their attention drawn to the matter in hand, it is usually too late. However, if the prospecting club is shrewd, they will continue putting in bids for their man, in spite of the increasingly irate denials from his Manager that he is up for sale.

On Loan

A variation on The Transfer is The Loan. This is when a club cannot afford to pay the full transfer fee for a player, so instead they take the player on loan for a specified period. It is also a useful way of giving youngsters who cannot get into the First team, League experience and it is a good method of farming out old veterans who threaten to spill all if placed on the transfer list. Some clubs are known as football graveyards, and a transfer there is regarded as the equivalent of being taken to the Knacker's Yard. It is a system that works almost entirely to the benefit of the wealthier clubs doing the lending. If the player suddenly blossoms out and starts to do well in his new surroundings, his own club will immediately recall the awkward little sod, and press him into service in their own team. If, however, he does badly while out on loan, he is allowed to finish his period away on loan, and on returning is loaned out three or four times again, to any comers, until he finally takes the hint.

Loaning is really very unfair because it means that clubs with a bit of money can get themselves out of short term difficulties while equally talented but less prosperous teams can suffer while opponents use a horde of rented players from higher divisions. There are several lower League clubs that make a practice of loaning players from higher divisions, because they have such bad teams themselves. Some of these teams, it is said by some sources, make a practice out of renting whole squads of First Division Substitutes and Reserves for the duration of the season. Anyone wishing to participate in this deplorable practice can do so by making contact with Uncle Harry, Consolidated Conmen, Bent Street, Soho.

A Change In The Action

Psychologists warn us that a constant change in a player's club can lead to dire personality and identity problems. It may, for example, take a sensitive Wing Half weeks if not months, to make the adjustment between environments. In the first place, he has to learn a whole new system of football. Some clubs prefer their players to do their fouling by elbowing, rather than by kicking opponents. Other clubs would never tolerate their players tripping up opponents, but are jealously proud of their Half Nelson, over-the-shoulder, two-arm double-strangle-hold. It can completely disrupt the carefully nurtured harmony of a football club, if a spoilsport Inside Right is bought, whose speciality is cracking people

UNCLE HARRY'S
SWOP SHOP
TODAY'S SPECIAL!
LET CONSOLIDATED CON-MEN WATCH OVER YOU!
H U
FOR SALE, RENT, LEASE, HIRE, TRANSFER, ...GIFT?
GOALIE WINGER BACK STRIKER REF.?
HARRY'S

across the shins with his boot, when the club has developed a world wide reputation for its elbowings in the groin. "Tradition's an important thing, you know", Chairman Knowlesworth-Blair told me, sipping from his balloon glass of Brandy, handed to him by his personal valet and constant companion, Miss Suzy Goodtime.

It *could* be said that whatever the outcome of Transfer Wrangles, the winners are always the players' Agents. If players do not move on to a new club, the club will generally grant the dissatisfied malcontent a renewed and better Contract, in order to stop the temptation arising again at a future date. Of course, we all know who will negotiate the renewed updated contract, and will take a renewed updated cut for himself . . .

And if the player does move on to a new club, this means that all his endorsements etc. have to be done again, with him wearing the strip of his new team. Which involves negotiations far too complex for the average footballer, but well within the scope of the average Agent.

However, all this may be doing Agents a grave injustice : as Honest Arthur, of Takeacut Ltd., Shoreditch, London, puts it : "Be reasonable! You've got to have the interests of the footballer at heart all the time, haven't you? Know what I mean? You can't expect an ordinary lad who has become a footballer by the assistance of his Agent, to handle his own £50,000 cut from his transfer, can you? I mean to say, I'm doing 'im a favour by taking half of it off his hands, ain't I?"

"*And as we move into extra time . . .*"